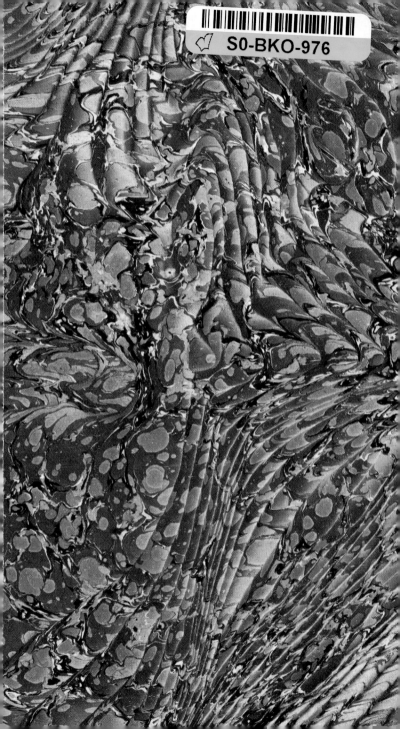

ON THE

DISCOVERY OF THE MISSISSIPPI,

AND ON

THE SOUTH-WESTERN, OREGON,
AND NORTH-WESTERN BOUNDARY

OF

THE UNITED STATES.

WITH

A TRANSLATION FROM THE ORIGINAL MS. OF MEMOIRS, ETC.
RELATING TO THE DISCOVERY OF THE MISSISSIPPI,
BY ROBERT CAVELIER DE LA SALLE AND THE CHEVALIER
HENRY DE TONTY.

By THOMAS FALCONER,

Of the Honourable Society of Lincoln's Inn.

A FACSIMILE REPRODUCTION
of the 1844 edition by
SHOAL CREEK PUBLISHERS, INC.

with an introduction by
Dr. Dorman H. Winfrey

Library of Congress Catalog Card No. 74-19562
ISBN No. 0-88319-020-6

PUBLISHER'S NOTE

For the bibliophiles among our readers, we'd like to let you know the qualities we have attempted to maintain for a true facsimile of the 1844 DISCOVERY OF THE MISSISSIPPI.

The original, from the Texas State Library Archives; though handled lovingly, shows signs of age and the "Marble Paper" on the front and back cover was worn through in several places. The inside back end sheet was in a good state of preservation, so it was reproduced for use as the front and back end sheets and for the cover.

The cover has been lithographed in four color process in order to produce as nearly as possible a close resemblance of the original edition.

The pagination may be misleading. It starts with the first five pages not paged, the first page number is page 6, being the second page of the text, and goes through page 96.

The second portion of the book, the "Memoir, Etc.", starts with no page numbers on the first three pages, then paging from 4 through 100. The "Petition" has no number, but the second and third pages bear page numbers 98 and 99. Also the "Errata" page is not numbered.

While this numbering system may seem a bit confusing, we thought you would prefer it, in its authenticity.

Shoal Creek Publishers, Inc.

INTRODUCTION

Thomas Falconer, born in Bath, England, on June 25, 1805, earned a place in English and Texas history by his writings on a wide range of subjects. He studied law in England and had a strong reputation in that country for his work in codifying the English laws and statutes.

In the spring of 1841 Falconer arrived in Texas, and in his *Notes of a Journey through Texas and New Mexico, in the Years 1841 and 1842* (1844) there is an account of his journey from Galveston to Austin by way of San Antonio. Falconer met President Mirabeau B. Lamar, and as "guest and scientific observer" joined the Texan Santa Fe Expedition along with George Wilkins Kendall of the New Orleans *Picayune*. Falconer kept a record of the expedition and in 1930 the materials were edited by F. W. Hodge and published under the title *Letters and Notes on the Texan Santa Fe Expedition, 1841-1842*. Hodge says Falconer "suffered with the rest without a whimper."

A second publication brought out in London in 1844 by Falconer is the present reprint, *On the Discovery of the Mississippi and on the South-Western, Oregon, and North-Western Boundary of the United States*. Some of the memoirs recorded by Falconer relate directly or indirectly to Texas, while the materials pertaining to La Salle were secured from the Archives of the Marine in 1843 when Falconer was in Paris. Colton Storm, compiler of *A Catalogue of the Everett D. Graff Collection of Western Americana* of the Newberry Library (1968) stated that "Falconer produced the first translation into English of La Salle's report and of* (Henri de) Tonty's *Memoire*, 1693."

One other publication by Falconer concerning the United States, *The Oregon Question*, was brought out in 1845. In addition to several published items relating to British law and the courts, Falconer compiled a valuable *Genealogy and Bibliography of the Falconer Family*, a copy of which belonged at one time to Texana collector Thomas W. Streeter. After serving some thirty years (1851-1881) as a judge Falconer died at Bath on August 28, 1882.

Although works by Falconer have been reprinted on several occasions (as have those of George Wilkins Kendall), so far as can be determined (*Guide to Reprints*) this is the first time *On the Discovery of the Mississippi and on the South-Western, Oregon, and North-Western Boundary of the United States* has been made available since the original printing in 1844. It should be greeted with applause from historians, librarians, collectors, and others. *American Book-Prices Current* listed a copy of the 1844 work selling in 1964 for $85.00.

Dorman H. Winfrey

Dorman H. Winfrey
Texas State Library

ON THE

DISCOVERY OF THE MISSISSIPPI,

AND ON

THE SOUTH-WESTERN, OREGON,

AND NORTH-WESTERN BOUNDARY

OF

THE UNITED STATES.

WITH

A TRANSLATION FROM THE ORIGINAL MS. OF MEMOIRS, ETC.
RELATING TO THE DISCOVERY OF THE MISSISSIPPI,
BY ROBERT CAVELIER DE LA SALLE AND THE CHEVALIER
HENRY DE TONTY.

By THOMAS FALCONER,

Of the Honourable Society of Lincoln's Inn.

LONDON:
SAMUEL CLARKE, 13 PALLMALL EAST.

1844.

LONDON:
PRINTED BY REYNELL AND WEIGHT,
LITTLE PULTENEY STREET.

PREFACE.

When at Paris, in 1843, I collected some materials to serve for an Account of the Discoveries of La Salle, and a friend was kind enough to give me copies of the documents I have translated, which had been obtained from the Archives of the Marine. In the course of the present year a 'Life of La Salle,' written by Mr Sparks, of Cambridge, Massachusetts, has been published; and this work renders any similar one needless. The documents I have translated—which I hope will hereafter be published in their original language — rendered an abstract of La Salle's journeys necessary, in order to explain their value ; but as those journeys have been the foundation of contested claims to extensive territories in North America, I enlarged my first sketch, and have traced their consequences in the negotiations that have occurred respecting the western boundary of the United States.

T. F.

October 25th, 1844.

DISCOVERY OF THE MISSISSIPPI,

ETC.

THE immediate result of the discoveries made in
North America by ROBERT CAVELIER DE LA SALLE
was the colonisation of the Mississippi by the French.
The merit of his exploration of this mighty river is
not obscured by the interest which attaches to the
narrative of the companions of Hernando de Soto, who
are supposed to have buried their adventurous leader
on its banks in the year 1542, and then, under the
guidance of Louis de Moscoso and Juan de Añasco,
to have sailed down it, and made their way to Mexico.
He was the first who traced the course of the
Mississippi from Canada to the sea, and he was the
first who sought the entrance of this great river from
the Gulf of Mexico. Though the object of his last
voyage was unsuccessful, his landing on the coast of
Texas has had as important an influence in the settlement of North America as his earlier discovery.

The memory of La Salle has been neglected by his
countrymen. The particulars of his personal history,

previous to his voyage down the Mississippi, are few. He was born at Rouen, he was educated in a seminary of the Jesuits, and he emigrated to Canada early in life. The date of his birth is unknown, and the fact of his having received a patent of nobility proves that he was of an obscure family.*

The earliest notice of him is perhaps contained in an MS. letter of M. Talon, Intendant of Canada, dated October, 1671, addressed to Colbert, in which it is simply mentioned that " the Sieur de la Salle had not yet returned from his expedition to the south of this country." He was therefore very early employed in the exploration of the country, and from his own memorial it appears that this was one of five ex-peditions which he made.

In 1675 he visited France, and received on the 13th of May in the same year a grant of the govern-ment and property of Fort Frontenac, which had been established under the name of Fort Cataraqui in 1672. He returned to Canada, and occupied himself in re-building the fort, substituting for earth and palisades, stone walls.

He returned again to France in 1677. On this occasion his title to Frontenac was confirmed by

---

* Mr Sparks says, " It does not appear in what rank or degree he was placed by this patent in the scale of titles." It is evident that he was merely placed in the rank of gentlemen, which was in France that of nobility. Charlevoix describes him to have been " d'une famille aisée."

letters patent, dated May 12, 1678, and he was commissioned to undertake the discovery of the Mississippi.
Having had an establishment at a place called La
Chine, on the island of Montreal, a little above the
Rapids, at the east end of Lake St Louis, it has been
inferred that he contemplated finding a route to China,
and that he sought unknown regions with wild and
indistinct ends. This, however, was not an inference
which the few facts known of him justified. Without
authority or commission he might have associated
himself with adventurers seeking fortune among
savages, and expecting wealth from the inhabitants
of the desert. But his expedition in 1671 was evidently under the authority of the government, and
was reported in the ordinary manner. The letters
patent of 1678 were issued with a distinct political
object; Louis XIV desired to attack the Spanish
possessions of America, and "had nothing more at
heart than to find a road to penetrate to them."* There
was no vision of a new world—of a traffic with China,
or of conquests of new nations, actuating the French
King. The settlers of Canada knew of many tribes
of Indians, but they were not decorated either with
gold or silver, and they could inform them of no

---

* A translation of these letters patent will be found at p. 18.
I was not aware until after I had printed it that they are to be
found in Le Clercq, vol. ii, p. 163. In Le Clercq the words
"notre pays" precede the words New France. I omitted them,
not being in my MS. copy of the original.

cities. The "El Dorado" of America was possessed by Spain, and France desired to seize the
prize. Colbert thought it "to be important for the
service and glory of the King to discover a port for
French vessels in the Gulf of Mexico." He wished
it to be "where the French might establish themselves,
and harass the Spaniards in the regions from whence
they drew their wealth."

With these objects, La Salle undertook to descend
the Mississippi. Marquette and Joliet had navigated
this river, as far south as the river Arkansas, in the
year 1673, until they reached "genial climes that have
almost no winter but rains, beyond the bound of the
Huron and Algonquin languages, to the vicinity of
the Gulf of Mexico, and to tribes of Indians that had
obtained European arms by traffic with Spaniards or
with Virginia." But no information existed of the
country south, of the windings of the river, of the
nations that dwelt on its banks, or the means of subsistence in a district so remote from the residence of
white men.*

Before La Salle left Paris he had the good fortune
to have had recommended to him, by the Prince de
Conti, the Chevalier Henry de Tonty, as a companion
in his undertaking. A cordial friendship was formed
between them, and there was no service required

---

* There is a very good notice of Marquette's discoveries in
the tenth volume of Mr Sparks's 'American Biography.'

which De Tonty does not appear to have performed with alacrity and with great courage.

La Salle and his companions left Rochelle on the 14th of July, 1678; they arrived at Quebec on the 15th of September following. They proceeded to Fort Frontenac, where they were joined by the Recollet fathers, Gabriel Louis Hennepin and Zenobe Membré, members of the order of St Francis.

The first object was to proceed to Niagara, in order to build a vessel above the Falls. Having stationed themselves there, and made arrangements to build it, La Salle left De Tonty in command with Father Hennepin, and returned to Fort Frontenac. On the 20th of January, 1679, La Salle came back. The materials which he had obtained for the completion of the vessel had been lost in the course of his journey, but after setting the work forward, he again left for Fort Frontenac. In his absence the building of the vessel proceeded, and was successfully launched; it was named the ' Griffin,' in honour of the Count de Frontenac, whose arms were supported by these heraldic animals. La Salle returned when all was prepared, and on the 7th of August, 1679, they were under sail on Lake Erie. De Tonty had been sent forward in a canoe to Detroit, and near this place was taken on board. The lake lying between Lakes Erie and Huron was named St Clair, after the saint to whom the day on which they entered it is dedicated.

They proceeded to an island at the mouth of Green

Bay, inhabited by the Pottawatimies : from thence to the Miamis river, since called the St Joseph, where La Salle built a fort. The vessel had been sent back to Niagara. Late in December they entered the Illinois country, crossing the portage from the lake to the Kankanee, the eastern branch of the Illinois river. The canoes were launched upon the water, and on the 1st of January, 1680, they reached the Lake Pimiteouy, since called Lake Peoria. Not far from hence Fort Crevecœur was built.

On the 29th of February, Father Hennepin was sent with the Sieur Dean (called Dacan, by Charlevoix, vol. i, p. 460), on an expedition to the Sioux. This was the termination of Hennepin's voyage with La Salle, and there can be no doubt that his narrative of occurrences, south of the Illinois, was fabricated by him.*

De Tonty was placed in the command of the fort, and La Salle resolved to travel overland with five men to Fort Frontenac, to obtain information of his vessel. He left in March, and discovering a spot which he considered to be favourable for the erection of a fort, sent orders to De Tonty to build one there. De Tonty proceeded to execute this order, but in his journey his men deserted. He was exposed to great danger from the Indians, and was wounded by them. He exhibited much coolness and presence of mind,

---

* Spark's 'Life of La Salle,' p. 78.

and managed to conciliate them. About this time Father Gabriel de la Ribourde was killed. After great difficulties they reached the village of the Pottawatimies, in November, 1680.

During the latter part of this year 1680, and the beginning of the year 1681, La Salle appears to have engaged in fruitless journeys to discover news of his vessel. In the middle of June, 1681, he met with De Tonty, and it was resolved that they should return back and make new preparations. After reaching Frontenac, M. La Salle proceeded to Montreal, and had an interview with the secretary of Count Frontenac on public affairs. At this place he made his will, which is dated August 11, 1681. Seventeen days subsequently, on August 28th, he left Frontenac with his company, and arrived at the Miamis river on the 3rd of November. His party at this time consisted of twenty-three Frenchmen, eighteen savages, Abenakis and Loups, ten Indian women, and three children. They crossed the portage at Chicagou to the Illinois river, and on the 6th of February, 1682, reached the Mississippi. On their course down the river they fell in with the Chicasaw Indians, whose practice of flattening the heads of their children is now perhaps only prevalent among a tribe living on the Columbia river, in the Oregon territory.

They reached the sea on the 7th of April, 1682, and formally took possession of the country, in the name of Louis XIV, on the 9th. The *Procès verbal* referred to in La Salle's Memoir is reprinted in the following pages. The country discovered is named Louisiana in this document, and as no earlier notice of the name is known, it was probably given by La Salle himself.

On their way back La Salle was seized with a dangerous illness, and De Tonty was sent forward to Michilimackinac. Father Zenobe remained, and slowly followed with him to the Miamis river, which they reached at the end of September. It was then determined that Zenobe should proceed to France with the news of the discovery, and he left the Miamis river for Quebec on the 8th of October.

La Salle remained in this part of the country until September of the next year (1683). There are three original letters written by him, respecting Indian affairs, in the Archives of the Marine:—one written at Fort St Louis, in the Illinois, dated April 2, 1683 ; another written at the portage of Chicagou, dated June 4, 1683, and another of great length, dated June 7, 1683. He left for Quebec in the autumn of the same year, and sailing for France, landed at Rochelle on the 18th of December.

From this delay of La Salle in the Illinois it is probable that he expected some news favourable to his own designs from France. But if this was so, it was prevented by the conduct of M. De la Barre, the new governor of Canada, who then, as in the case of governors in later times, was pleased to represent the sincere efforts of Canadians to advance the welfare of the province as exhibiting disloyal pretensions. He was accused of acting the part of a sovereign, and of oppressing his countrymen. De Tonty very quietly alludes to the matter, and merely remarks that La Salle was on his way to Quebec before an order directing him to come there was received. M. De la Barre little understood the extension of the interests, and the growing claims of the province he governed. These were fortunately better known in France, and he was displaced. M. Denonville was appointed to succeed him.

La Salle arrived in France shortly after the death of Colbert, whose son, Seignelay, was Minister of Marine. Two memoirs which he delivered are printed in the following pages, and they are the first papers, written by La Salle, that have yet been published, and their existence has been hitherto unknown. In one he gives an account of the country south of the Mississippi, very slightly alluding to the reports which had been circulated against him. In the other, which is printed first, he urges an expedition by sea to the Mississippi, and accompanies it with a note of the equipment and supplies requisite to undertake it. In this memoir he confirms a statement of Hennepin, which has often been questioned, of his desire to seize the mines of Saint Barbe, while at the same time he alludes to the possibility of opening a passage to the South Sea.

The application of La Salle was acceded to, and he was authorised to form a colony on the south of the Mississippi.

When preparing to sail he was again fortunate in obtaining a companion no less faithful in his friendship, and active and useful to him, than De Tonty had been. When at Rouen, Joutel, a native of Rouen, and who had just returned to that city after sixteen years' service in the army, applied for permission to accompany him. This was assented to, and Joutel ultimately became the historian of the expedition.

The expedition sailed July 24th, 1684. It was composed of four vessels: the ' Joly,' of thirty-six guns, commanded by M. De Beaujeu; the ' Belle,' of six guns; the 'Aimable,' belonging to Massiot, a merchant of Rochelle, and commanded by M. Aigron ; and a small vessel of thirty tons, freighted with stores and ammunition for St Domingo.

Including the crews, 280 persons embarked in these vessels, among whom were Zenobe Membré, (sometimes called Zenoble) who had accompanied La Salle down the Mississippi ; Anastase Douay, Maxime Le Clercq, and Denys Marquet ; but the last was afterwards put ashore, on account of illness, before leaving the coast of France. There were with them three priests : Cavelier, brother of La Salle, Chefdeville, a relative, and Majulle, ecclesiastics of St

Sulpice. Also, Cavelier and Moranget, nephews of La Salle, the Marquis of Sabloniere, a Canadian family of the name of Talon, and 100 soldiers, and some young women.

After sailing, an injury to the bowsprit of the 'Joly' compelled them to return and put into the port of Rochfort. They sailed again August 1, 1684. The voyage to the Gulf of Mexico was not unfavourable, though disagreements between La Salle and Beaujeu occurred.* By some letters of Beaujeu, lately printed for the first time, he expressed his ill-will towards La Salle before he sailed. He asked, " to be permitted to take great credit to himself for consenting to obey the orders of La Salle;" "that no operation of war should be undertaken without consulting him;" and stated that " it was disagreeable to him to be under the orders of La Salle, who had no military rank." The feelings thus early exhibited were in active operation in the course of the voyage. Another letter of M. De Beaujeu, dated October 20, states : " If the Sieur De la Salle shall not recover, I shall pursue different measures from those which he has adopted, which I do not approve of. Nor can I comprehend how a man should dream of settling a country surrounded by Spaniards and Indians with a company of workmen and women instead of soldiers. But I shall undertake nothing

---

* See 'Life' by Mr Sparks, 116, 117, 122, 123.

without the consent of the Governor and Intendant, whose counsels I shall follow."

After passing Cuba, and making towards the coast where they expected to discover the Mississippi, they came into soundings in December. They believed the current of the gulf stream had carried them too far east, when, in fact, they had passed the river. They kept on to the west until all were satisfied they had continued this course too far; an opinion entertained by La Salle some time before, in opposition to Beaujeu. They therefore returned along the coast, and entered the Bay of St Bernard, called by La Salle the Bay of St Louis, and supposed to have been Matagorda Bay. There were two channels into the bay, and an island between them. The pilot reported favourably, but in the attempt to bring in the 'Aimable,' it was lost. In March Beaujeu sailed for France. He had landed eight cannon, and took back the balls under the pretence that he could not disturb the cargo of his vessel. The 'Belle' was left with the colonists.

The first object of La Salle was to build a fort, and this having been done, he left in March with fifty men to find the lost river, leaving 130 persons in the fort under the command of Joutel. In this journey he found a better position for a fort on a river which he named Vaches, on account of the number of buffaloes seen near it. Seventy men, women, and children removed to this place. In July the old fort, which had been left occupied by thirty men, was abandoned. When Joutel joined La Salle he found affairs in a miserable state. Within a short time thirty of the company had died. The master carpenter had been lost in wandering from the camp, and his duties had been undertaken by La Salle himself, who marked out the tenons and mortices of the timbers, and directed the works. But the fort was completed, and afforded a sufficient protection to the party.

"This, it is said, (' Bancroft's History of America,' vol. iii, p. 171), was the settlement which made Texas a part of Louisiana. In its sad condition, it had yet saved from the wreck a good supply of arms and bars of iron for the forge. Even now the colony possessed, from the bounty of Louis XIV, more than was contributed by all the English monarchs together for the twelve English colonies on the Atlantic. Its number still exceeded that of the colony of Smith of Virginia, or of those who embarked in the 'Mayflower.' France took possession of Texas ; her arms were carved on its stately forest trees ; and by no treaty or public document, except the general cession of Louisiana, did she ever after relinquish the right to the province as colonised under her banners, and made more surely a part of her territory, because the colony found there its grave."

In October La Salle left the fort in search of the Mississippi, in company with twenty men, leaving Joutel in command. The ' Belle ' was directed to proceed along the coast, and his papers and equipage were put on board it. Sickness appears to have made terrible ravages, for thirty-four persons only, including women and children, are represented as having been left with Joutel.

At the end of four months La Salle returned. He had reason to be satisfied that the ' Belle' had been lost, and determined on an expedition to communicate, if possible, with Canada. Twenty men were selected to accompany him, and he left on the 22nd of April, 1686. The fort was confided to the care of Joutel, and a few days after La Salle had left, some of the crew of the ' Belle' arrived, who confirmed the loss of the vessel.

La Salle, after proceeding as far as the Cenis, on the Trinity river, found himself compelled by sickness and desertion to return again to the Vaches, and arrived there on the 17th of October.

Another expedition was then resolved on, and either seventeen or twenty men were selected for it, among whom were Joutel, Father Anastase, Cavelier the Priest, and young Cavelier, Moranget, Duhaut, L'Archevêque, Hiens, Liotot, Talon, Teissier, Saget, and an Indian named Nika.*

---

* De Tonty speaks of an Englishman as one of the number, but Charlevoix says (vol. ii, p. 22) : " Quélques uns le nomment ' Jemme,' et disent que c'etoit un soldat Anglois ; mais il y a bien d'apparence qu'ils se trompent." ' Jimmy' certainly sounds very English.

The fort was placed under the command of Barbier, and there remained with him Father Zenobe, of whose ultimate fate nothing is known, Maxime, Chefdeville, Sabloniere, and others, amounting to twenty persons, seven of whom were women and girls; so that at this time only about forty were surviving of the 180 persons who landed in Texas.

On the 12th of January, 1687, La Salle and his companions left the fort. It was a season of the year ill suited for the enterprise, for in Texas it is not until the end of March that a journey of this nature, even with horses, can be exempt from great difficulties. About the middle of March they came near the Cenis. At this point of the journey a conspiracy was formed to assassinate La Salle. On the 20th of March, 1687, Moranget, the nephew of La Salle, together with Saget and the faithful Indian Nika, were killed by Duhaut, Liotot, Hiens, and L'Archevêque. The men not coming up, La Salle himself went to search after them. As he approached the assassins, he asked after his nephew, when he was instantly shot. " Te voila, grand Bacha, te voila !" was the revengeful exclamation of joy as one of the men looked on his dead body.

"Thus perished," says Father Anastase, "our wise conductor, constant in adversities, intrepid, generous, engaging, adroit, skilful, and capable of anything. He who, during a period of twenty years, had softened the fierce temper of a vast number of savage nations,

was massacred by his own people. He died in the vigour of life, in the midst of his career and labours, without the consolation of having seen their results."*
But Joutel, after acknowledging his great capacity and ability, his firmness and courage, and his indefatigable labour, which might have procured for him a glorious issue of his great undertaking, adds, that "these merits were counterbalanced by a haughtiness of manner which often made him unbearable, and by a harshness towards those under his command which drew on him an implacable hatred, and was the cause of his death."

After this sad event seven of the party, including Anastase, Joutel, Cavelier the Priest, Cavelier the younger, De Marle, Teissier, and Bartholemy, proceeded together towards Canada. On the 24th of June, on reaching the Mississippi, near the junction of the Arkansas, they saw with great gladness a large cross and a house, where Tonty had left six men, probably in the hope of communicating with La Salle. Two of the men, Contour and Delaunay, alone remained, the other four having gone back to the Illinois. From hence they pursued their journey, and on the 14th of September reached Fort St Louis, in the Illinois.

The direction of La Salle's route has been the subject of some comment; but Mr Sparks correctly

---

* Le Clercq, vol. ii, 340.

observes, "That scarcely a fact connected with his discoveries is more demonstrable than that he never went a day's journey from the Bay of St Bernard towards Mexico; and that all his travels were eastward, in the direction of the Mississippi or of the Illinois."

De Tonty was found stationed at St Louis. From the first moment he heard of the expedition he had endeavoured to assist La Salle. In the spring of 1686 he sailed down the Mississippi, and a second time reached the sea. He sent canoes to the east and the west, and vainly sought his old companion and friend. On returning, he complied with the request of some of his men to settle on the Arkansas, and it was the sight of this settlement that assured the survivors of La Salle of their safety.

Probably for the purpose of securing La Salle's property, his brother Cavelier told De Tonty that La Salle was alive, and obtained from him about 28*l.* sterling. The statement that he practised a fraud by presenting a letter signed by La Salle is not confirmed by De Tonty, and is no doubt a fabrication.

In the spring of 1688 Cavelier left Fort St Louis, and proceeded to Quebec, which he reached in August. He sailed for France, and arriving at Rochelle, October the 9th, gave the first intelligence of the disasters that had occurred and the mournful particulars of the death of La Salle.

The fate of the persons left by La Salle in Texas is related by Charlevoix (vol. ii, pp. 39, 40).

"The Spaniards of New Mexico, alarmed at the enterprise of La Salle, were resolved to spare nothing to check it. Five hundred men were sent to the Cenis, who found upon their arrival only a man named L'Archevêque, and a sailor of Rochelle, whom they made prisoners. It is not known if these two persons knew of the death of La Salle, but it is certain that after a short time other Spaniards met with Munier and Talon, brother of the Talons who had been made prisoners by the Clamcoets, who took them to a settlement of the Cenis, where they were well treated. The soldiers had in their company some Franciscans, whom they wished to settle among the Indians; and knowing that the two Frenchmen, who well understood the language, might be useful to the missionaries, on this account treated them mildly, in order to obtain their services. Talon trusted them, and informed them that his brothers and his sister were slaves among the Clamcoets. A company of soldiers was sent; but this detachment could only bring back the two Talons, their sister, and the Italian; their masters, who entertained towards them much regard, having released them with regret. In the following year two hundred and fifty Spaniards came to the same settlement, and found there Jean Baptist Talon and Breman. They carried them first to St Louis Potosi, and then to Mexico, with the other two Talons and their sister, and the Viceroy took them into his service.

" L'Archevêque and Grollet were first carried to Spain, and then sent back to Mexico, apparently to labour in the mines. The Italian was sent to Vera Cruz, and was shut up in a prison, which probably he never left unless to be condemned to the same labour. Nothing is known of the fate of Breman. Perhaps he was permitted to join the Talons, for the favour the three brothers obtained is attributed to their age, which prevented their obtaining any great knowledge of the country, whilst the others were grown-up men, who might have given information in France upon all they might have observed in their expeditions.

" Eight years afterwards the two elder Talons, being of age to bear arms, were enrolled in the fleet, and embarked in the ' Christo,' bearing the flag of the Vice Admiral. This vessel was taken in 1696 by the Chevalier des Angiers, and the two brothers, thus recovering their liberty, returned to France, where they themselves related these particulars. Afterwards the Viceroy of Mexico, who had retained near him the youngest Talon and his sister, took them with him on his return to Spain."

De Tonty, with the bravery which distinguished him, attempted to save this party. In 1689 he for the third time descended the Mississippi, and knowing that they were to the west he ascended the Red River. After every effort to reach them, the desertion of his men compelled him to abandon the attempt.

These were the first measures of the French to colonise the southern district of the Mississippi. Their failure and the disastrous events which accompanied them, did not, however, deter the French government in its pursuit of this object. In 1697 the illustrious Canadian D'Iberville was commissioned to sail to the Gulf of Mexico, and to make a settlement on the Mississippi. He made the voyage successfully, and returned to France.* Other voyages were subsequently

---

* I do not know if there is any published account of this family. The following particulars of the children of Charles Lemoyne, Seignor of Longueil, who settled in Lower Canada in 1640, are taken from a paper in the Archives of the Marine at Paris :—

I. Sieur Charles Lemoyne, Baron de Longueil, was "Lieutenant de Roi de la Ville et Gouvernment de Montreal." He served in Canada as Captain of Marine. He was wounded in the attack of the English on Quebec in 1690, and in a conflict with the Iroquois at Lachine his arm was broken. He was created Baron de Longueil by letters patent, when the seignory of Longueil was also erected into a barony. — " Nous avons cru qu'il etait de notre justice de donner non seulement à sa terre et seigneurie de Longueil un titre d'honneur mais encor â sa personne quelques marques d'une distinction honorable qui passe à la posterité et qui soit un sujêt d'une loiable emulation à ses enfans pour les engager à suivre son exemple." The letters patent state that he was to take rank with other barons of France.

II. Le Sieur Jacques Lemoyne de Saint Helene, the second son, a captain of a company of marine. He was killed

made by him,—a colony was planted and left in charge of his brother Bienville. " Some of the

---

in the attack of the English on Quebec in October, 1690.—(See Bancroft's ' History of America,' vol. iii, p. 185.) The attack was made by an expedition sent from Massachusetts, and on its failure the yearly festival of our Lady of Victory was established in the church of the lower town of Quebec.— (Le Clercq, vol. ii, p. 457.)

III. SIEUR —— LEMOYNE D'IBERVILLE, the most illustrious of the brothers. He was born in 1662. In 1686 he was sent by M. Denonville, Governor of Canada, together with his brother St Helene, on an expedition to Hudson's Bay, under the command of M. De Troyes. He was made the commander of a fort established in this expedition. While stationed here he captured an English vessel, and received the especial thanks of the Governor for his conduct in this post. By a commission of the 9th of June, 1687, his authority was extended over the whole district of Hudson's Bay. In 1689 he took some English vessels, and again received the especial thanks of the Governor. In 1691 he went to France, and in the following year was made captain of a frigate. By his instructions, dated April 11, 1692, he was to convoy some vessels to Canada, and was then to make an attack on Fort Bourbon, a fort established by the French in 1681, and taken by the English in 1683. The vessels convoyed arrived in safety, but the voyage having been long, the season did not permit an attempt to be made on Fort Bourbon. In cruising, however, off the coast of New England, he captured a colonial armed vessel. Unfavourable weather had delayed the execution of the design against Fort Bourbon; but he successfully attacked it in 1694, when his brother Louis de Chateauguay was killed. In 1696 and 1697 he distinguished himself in attacks on the English settlements. On his return to France, at the end of the year of 1697, he was commissioned to sail to the

B

colonists perished for want of enterprise, some from
climate ; others prospered from their indomitable

Gulf of Mexico, in order to discover the entrance of the Mississippi from the sea. He sailed in 1698, and after a successful
voyage entered the great river on the 17th of October. He
afterwards ascended it a hundred leagues ; and " a parish and
a bayou that bear the name of Iberville mark the route of his
return through the lakes which he named Maurepas and Pontchartrain." After establishing a fort he returned to France.
He was made a knight of the Order of St Louis on account of
this success, and M. Ponchartrain assured him in a letter dated
August 26, 1699, "that he would lose no occasion to render
him any good service in his power." Instructions to sail again
to the Mississippi were issued September 22, 1699, directing
him to survey the country discovered, to seek for mines, and to
establish settlements. This voyage was successful, and he returned to France in 1700. Instructions for his third voyage
were dated August 27, 1701, and he returned to France in June,
1702. According to a letter of M. Ponchartrain, dated October 15, 1703, he was to have been employed in an expedition to
the coast of New England, which was abandoned on account of
the difficulties of the government. When about to sail a fourth
time to the Mississippi, at the end of the year 1704, he was
taken seriously ill at Rochelle, and was unable to leave France
until 1706. He had laid the foundation of a great city in the
New World which he was not destined again to reach. He
died at Havannah, July 9, 1706. He left a widow, "Dame
Bethune," and four children.

IV. Sieur Paul Lemoyne de Maricour, captain of a company of marine. He served under his brother D'Iberville He
died from illness occasioned by exhaustion and fatigue in an
expedition against the Iroquois.

V. Sieur —— Lemoyne de Serigny.—He served under his
brother D'Iberville in all his expeditions, and died at New
Orleans.

energy. The Canadian Du Tissenet, purchasing a compass, and taking an escort of fourteen Canadians, went fearlessly from Dauphine Island by way of the

---

VI. Sieur ——— Lemoyne Bienville, an officer of marine. He was killed at a place called Repintigny by the Iroquois, who surrounded and burnt the house in which he and others were, none escaping.

VII. Sieur Louis Lemoyne de Chateauguay. — He was killed by the English at Fort Bourbon, in 1694.

VIII. Sieur ——— Lemoyne d'Assigny.—He died at Saint Domingo, where his brother was compelled to leave him on account of sickness, in the course of the voyage to the Mississippi, in 1701.

IX. Antoine Lemoyne.—Died young.

X. Sieur ——— Lemoyne Bienville.—He accompanied his brother D'Iberville on his first voyage in 1698, and was left in command of the colony. In a memorial, dated New Orleans, January 25, 1723, he set forth his services, and described himself " Chevalier de l'ordre militaire de St Louis et Commandant General de la Province de la Louisianne ; " and states that, of eleven sons, four were at that time alive, who were " decorés de la croix de St Louis." He explored the country to a considerable distance from the river, and was eminently successful in his administration of public affairs. He founded New Orleans. For a time he ceased to be Governor, but after the failure of Law's Mississippi scheme, he again held the office.

XI. Sieur Jean Baptiste Lemoyne de Chateauguay.— He was captain of a company of marine in Louisiana.

There appear, therefore, to have been two brothers who took the name of Bienville, and two of the name of Chateauguay.

There were two sisters, one of whom married the Sieur de

Mobile River to Quebec, and returned to the banks of the Mississippi with his family. The most successful colonists of Louisiana were the hardy emigrants from Canada, who brought with them little beyond a staff and the coarse clothes that covered them."—(Bancroft, vol. iii, p. 352.) But the "occupation of Louisiana was esteemed an encroachment on Spanish territory," and before the arrival of D'Iberville "the Fort of Pensacola had been established by three hundred Spaniards from Vera Cruz. This prior occupa-

---

Noyan, and the other the Sieur de la Chassagne, a major of marines.

The only known representative of this illustrious family is the Baron Grant of Longueil, in Lower Canada, who, through the female line, inherited the barony. It is not clear that personal honours under the French law would descend through a female, but the letters patent created a territorial title. The honour gives no precedence among British subjects, and colonial honours have never been favoured by the English Government, our colonial system, in America, having formerly been eminently democratic. It was otherwise with the French Government. In 1667 the Intendant, M. Talon, writing to Colbert, states, that the nobility of Canada consisted of four nobles of an early creation, and of four who had received letters of nobility in the previous year ; and he recommends that eight more should be added to the number.—(MS). On October 2, 1671, M. Talon, in another letter to Colbert, writes, that he had received ten medals from the King to be conferred on persons who had distinguished themselves in the colony ; and at the same time thanks him for the letters of nobility by which "La terre des Islets" had been erected into a barony in his favour.

tion is the reason why, afterwards, Pensacola remained a part of Florida, and the dividing line between that province and Louisiana was drawn between the bays of Pensacola and Mobile."—(Bancroft, vol. iii, pp. 347—200.)

The last that is known of the brave and generous De Tonty is, that he joined D'Iberville at the mouth of the Mississippi, about the year 1700, and that two years afterwards he was employed on a mission to the Chicasaws. When D'Iberville reached the river, a letter written by De Tonty, fourteen years before, and which had been preserved by the Indians, was delivered to him. It was addressed to La Salle, and Charlevoix has preserved it. It was as follows :—

" At the village of Quinipessas, April 20, 1685 (1686). Sir,—Having found the column on which you placed the arms of France overthrown by the driftwood floated down by the stream, I caused a new one to be erected about seven leagues from the sea, where I left a letter suspended on a tree. All the nations have sung the calumet. These people greatly fear us since your attack on their village. I close by saying that it gives me great uneasiness to be obliged to return under the misfortune of not having found you. Two canoes have examined the coast thirty leagues towards Mexico, and twenty-five towards Florida."

Such were the events which gave Louisiana to the French.

The publications which contain a narrative of the voyages of La Salle, are those of De Tonty, Le Clercq, Joutel, Hennepin, and Charlevoix.

The title of the work published in De Tonty's name is :—

" Dernieres Découvertes dans l'Amerique Septentrionale de M. de la Salle. Mises au jour par M. le Chevalier Tonti, Gouverneur du Fort Saint Louis, aux Illinois." Paris, 1697.

This has hitherto been the chief authority respecting the voyage down the Mississippi, but Charlevoix says that Tonty disavowed the publication, declaring that it did him no honour in any particular. Mr Bancroft calls it, " a legend full of geographical contradictions, of confused dates, and manifest fiction." And Mr Sparks speaks of it " as a work not to be trusted as a record of historical facts, and that it is probable that De Tonty's notes fell into the hands of a writer in Paris, who held a ready pen, and was endowed with a most fertile imagination, and that he infused his own inventions so copiously into the text of De Tonty, that the task would now be utterly hopeless, of selecting the true from the false, except so far as any particular passage may be confirmed by other authorities."

In this volume the narrative of De Tonty for the first time appears in its original form. It confirms the accuracy of the remarks of Mr Sparks, respecting the great and extravagant additions that were made to it in the published work, in which events were transposed, geographical descriptions misplaced, and at least two-thirds of fiction added. It is, therefore, needless to point out what portions of it the original narrative does not confirm. But the errors of date in the published work are to be found in the original. Thus, 1679 is written by mistake for 1680 (p. 53); the *fête Dieu*, in June, 1681, is placed in October (p. 61); June 1683 for 1682 (p. 74)—and these mistakes run throughout the narrative, though the facts appear to be recited in their proper order. All that was known of De Tonty reflected the highest honour on him. He must be ranked next to La Salle, among those who contributed to the extension of the western settlement of Canada, and to his bold and repeated excursions down the Mississippi, the successful expedition of D'Iberville must be ascribed. Whatever doubt the failure of the first expedition to the Gulf of Mexico may have produced in France, must have been removed by the information obtained through his courageous efforts to save his countrymen. His memory has suffered, for nearly a century and a half, under the reproach of his supposed want of veracity, and from this it will be hereafter exempt.

The work of Le Clercq consists of two small volumes. The title of it is :—

" Premier Establissement de la Foy dans la Nouvelle France, contenant la publication de l'Evangile, l'histoire des Colonies Francoises et les fameuses découvertes depuis le Fleuve de Saint Laurent, la Louissiane et le Fleuve Colbert, jusq'au Golphe Mexique, achevées sous la conduite de feu Monsieur de la Salle, par ordre du Roi; avec les victoires remportées en Canada, par les armes de Sa Majesté, sur les Anglois et les Iroquois on 1690. Par le père Chrestien LE CLERCQ, Missionaire Recollet de la Province de Saint Antoine de Pade en Arthois, Gardien des Recollets de Lens." Paris, 1691, 2 vols.

The chapters in the second volume, relating to the journies of La Salle, are brief but very interesting. The account of the first expedition was derived from the missionary Recollet, Father Zenobe ; of the second from Father Anastase.

The fullest account of La Salle's second expedition was written by Joutel, whose Christian name does not appear to be known. It is entitled :—

" Journal Historique du Dernier Voyage que feu M. de la SALLE, fit dans le Golfe de Mexique, pour trouver l'embouchure et le cours de la Rivière de Missicipi, nommée à présent la Riviere de Saint Louis, que traverse la Louisiane. Où l'on voit l'histoire tragique de sa mort et pleusieurs choses curieuses du nouveau monde. Par Monsieur JOUTEL, l'un des compagnons de ce voyage; redigé et mis en ordre par Monsieur DE MICHEL." Paris, 1713.

Joutel was more fortunate in his editor than De Tonty. His narrative may be most implicitly relied on, even in the few particulars in which he differs from Father Anastase. His account of Texas is brief, and yet he tells almost all that any other than a scientific traveller could relate of its flat lands, open prairies, and narrow belts of timber on the borders of its rivers. Any person who has visited that country, will admit that he told nothing but what he actually saw of it, and on this account, independently of other reasons, will readily trust his relation of personal facts.

Hennepin accompanied La Salle to the Illinois, and there parted from him. His account of the Mississippi south of this river is a mere fabrication, and the criticism of Mr Sparks (Life of La Salle, p. 78) to prove it such, is conclusive.

Charlevoix's great work 'Histoire et Description Generale de la Nouvelle France,' &c. Paris, 3 vols., 4to., 1744, supplies many facts necessary to complete the history of La Salle's discoveries, and no doubt has been expressed of their accuracy.

The papers of La Salle in this volume are the first which have been printed. They set at rest the speculations which have been indulged in respecting the object of his travels. But other papers than these exist, and it is to be hoped that they will be collected and published with the narrative of De Tonty and a new edition of the works of Joutel and Le Clercq. It will be an undertaking that can only be executed in Paris, and will be the best memorial his countrymen can offer to atone for their unaccountable neglect of his memory and of the records of his great public services.

Louisiana remained a French colony until 1763. By the treaty of Paris of the 10th of February of that year, made between England, France, and Spain, the countries of Nova Scotia, Canada, and Cape Breton, were ceded to England, and the limits of the remaining French settlements on the west "were irrevocably fixed by a line drawn along the middle of the river Mississippi from its source to the river Iberville, and from thence by a line drawn along the middle to this river and the Lakes Maurepas and Ponchartrain to the sea." The river and Fort of Mobile, and everything which France possessed on the left bank of the Mississippi being ceded, "except the town of New Orleans and the island on which it is situated."

By the 20th article of the same treaty Spain ceded to England, Florida with Fort St Augustin and the Bay of Pensacola and all that it possessed on the continent of North America to the east, or south-east of the river Mississippi.

By a secret treaty of Nov. 3, 1762, signed the same day on which the preliminaries of peace between Great Britain, France, and Spain were signed,— France ceded to Spain "all the country known under the name of Louisiana, as also New Orleans and the island in which that city is situated"—that is, so much of Louisiana as had not been agreed to be transferred by France to Great Britain.

On the 3rd of September, 1783, by the treaty made with Spain, East and West Florida were ceded by Great Britain. Spain thus became again possessed of these its ancient colonies.

By the treaty also made on the 3rd of September, 1783, between Great Britain and the United States of America, the independence of these states was recogised, and their north-western, western, and southern boundaries were thus described:—" By a line through the middle of Lake Erie until it arrives at the water communication between that lake and Lake Huron; thence along the middle of the said water communication into the Lake Huron; thence, through the middle of the said lake to the water communication between that lake and Lake Superior; thence through Lake Superior, northward of the Isles Royal and Philipeaux, to the Long Lake; thence, through the middle of Long Lake and the water between it and the Lake of the Woods, to the Lake of the Woods; thence through the said lake to the most north-western point thereof; and from thence, on a due west course, to the river Mississippi; thence, by a line drawn along the middle of the said river Mississippi, until it shall intersect the northernmost part of the 31st degree of north latitude—south, by a line to be drawn due east from the determination of the line last mentioned in the latitude 31 degrees north of the equator to the middle of the river Apalachiola or Catahouche; thence along the middle thereof to its junction with the Flint river; thence straight to the head of the St Mary's River, and thence along the middle of the St Mary's River to the Atlantic Ocean."

There was one error in this otherwise clearly defined boundary :—the head waters of the Mississippi river are south of the Lake of the Woods, and consequently a line due west from the lake would not touch the river. The clear intention of both parties was to terminate the boundary where this junction was expected to take place—where, if the Mississippi had continued in a course N. it would have intersected the line running due W. from the Lake of the Woods. This obvious correction of the mistake is adopted in the map lately published in America by Mr Greenhow, in which a dotted line from the head waters of the Mississippi to the line running due W. of the Lake of the Woods completes this boundary. But nothing W. or N. of this line was granted by Great Britain to the United States in 1783, and nothing N. of the head waters of the Mississippi was retained by France under the treaty of 1763. This, it will presently be shown, it is material to observe.

On October 1, 1800, Louisiana was retro-ceded by

Spain to France " with the same extent that it now has in the hands of Spain, and that it had when France possessed it, and such as it should be after the treaties subsequently entered into between Spain and other states." It was an act of retro-cession, but it transferred so much less than France originally held, as had been shorn from it by the treaty of 1763, which gave to Great Britain, and through Great Britain to the United States, nearly the entire eastern bank of the Mississippi.

In 1803 France sold Louisiana to the United States for eleven million of dollars. The purchase included all lands " on the east side of the Mississippi river not then belonging to the United States, as far as the great chain of mountains which divide the waters running into the Pacific and those falling into the Atlantic Ocean; and from the said chain of moun-tains to the Pacific Ocean, between the territory claimed by Great Britain on one side and by Spain on the other."*—(History of the Federal Government, by Alden Bradford, Boston, 1840, p. 130.) No point was mentioned where the line in the chain of moun-tains was to commence, nor where the tract of land lay, forming a portion of Louisiana, lying between the territory claimed by Spain and Great Britain. France had nothing to sell but what constituted Louisiana after the cession made to Great Britain in 1763.

---

* Mr Greenhow in his elaborate work on the Oregon question, has omitted all notice of this very important passage.

There was, nevertheless, inserted in this treaty of sale a reference to a perfectly undefined line to the Pacific, having no defined point of commencement, and referring to territory having no definable boundary either on the north, or the south, or on the east.

The above is an abstract of the events connected with the discovery, occupation, and settlement of Louisiana, and of its transfer to the United States. It is now proposed to give an outline of the discussions which have occurred respecting the measures taken by the United States to define the limits of its purchase; first, noticing those with Spain which terminated in the settlement of the Mexican or south-western boundary; secondly, those still pending respecting the Oregon or western boundary; and lastly, those affecting the north-western boundary.

The treaty for the purchase of Louisiana was not completed when President Jefferson, in a letter, dated August 12, 1803, wrote thus to Mr Breckenridge :—" The boundary which I deem not admitting question are the high lands on the western side of the Mississippi, inclosing all its waters—the Missouri, of course—and terminating in the line drawn from the north-western point, from the Lake of the Woods to the nearest source of the Mississippi, as lately settled between Great Britain and the United States. We have some claims to extend on the sea-coast westwardly to the Rio Norte or Bravo—and better to go eastwardly to the Rio Perdido between Mobile and Pensacola, the ancient boundary of Louisiana."

It is evident, therefore, that at this time it was not contemplated to demand any line running beyond the mountains on the west. The claim to the whole of Texas, which the line proposed to be drawn along the Rio del Norte would have included, was founded on the discoveries of La Salle. It is an opinion then and still entertained in America, that Louisiana included this country, as the following passages from Mr Bancroft's ' History of the United States' prove: —" Such were the events (La Salle's expedition, &c.) which gave to France not only New France and Acadia, Hudson's Bay, and Newfoundland, but a claim to a moiety of Maine, of Vermont, and to more than a moiety of New York, to the whole valley of the Mississippi, and to Texas, even as far as the Rio Bravo del Norte."—(Vol. iii, c. xxi, p. 175.) " Louisiana, on the side of Spain, at the west and south, was held to extend to the River del Norte; and on the map published by the French Academy, the line passing from that river to the river that divides it from Red River, followed that ridge to the Rocky Mountains, and then descended to seek its termination in the Gulf of California. On the Gulf of Mexico, it is certain that France claimed to the Del Norte."—(Vol. iii, p. 343.) " During the period of hostility (1720), La Harpe in a letter to the nearest Spanish governor,

had claimed 'Texas to the Del Norte as part of Louisiana.' France was too feeble to stretch its colonies
far to the west, but its rights were esteemed so clear
that in time of peace the attempt to occupy the
country was renewed. This second attempt of Bernard de la Harpe to plant a colony near the Bay of
Matagorda, had no other result than to incense the
natives against the French, and to stimulate the
Spaniards to the occupation of the country by a fort.
Yet the French ever regarded the mouth of Del
Norte as the western limit of Louisiana, on the Gulf
of Mexico, and English geography (Pople's Map) recognised the claim."—(Vol. iii, p. 353; also pp.
171, 175.)

The frequent repetition of this opinion, which is
very generally prevalent in the United States, by so
able an historian as Mr Bancroft, could only have
arisen from a very strong impression of what he believed to have been the former limits of Louisiana.
In adopting it he has fallen into an error, which an
accurate notice of the facts would have prevented.

In 1804 a negotiation took place between the government of the United States and Spain, to deter-
mine the southern-western boundary of Louisiana;
but the claims of the former were regarded to be in-
admissible, and the pretensions of the one country
and the demands of the other were so opposed, that
the discussions were broken off.

In 1819, Don Louis de Onis was commissioned, on

the part of Spain, to renew the negotiation. (' Official Correspondence between Don Louis de Onis, Minister for Spain to the United States, and of John Quincy Adams, Secretary of State, in relation to the Floridas, and the Boundary of Louisiana.' London, 1818). On the part of America it was contended that Texas was part of Louisiana. The evidence in support of the claim was the discovery of the Mississippi, throughout its whole length in 1682 ; the landing of La Salle in Matagorda Bay, in 1685; a grant made by Louis XIV to Crozat; a memoir said to have been written by Vergennes in the reign of Louis XVI ; a chart of Louisiana, by Lopez, published in 1762; a map of De Lisle of the Academy of Sciences at Paris, revised and republished in 1782 ; a map published at Nuremberg in 1712 ; an " Atlas Geographicus " published in London in 1717 ; what is called an official British map, published in 1755; the narratives of Hennepin, Tonty, and Joutel; a letter of La Harpe, dated July 8, 1719; an order from Bienville to La Harpe, dated August 12, 1721, and a geographical work of Don Antonio de Alcedo, published in Spain.

The far greater part of this evidence was utterly irrelevant. All the maps mentioned are unofficial. A British map, official or non-official, could have no authority in determining rights dependent on the claims of France or Spain. The map makers of London, and the map-maker of Nuremberg, must be

put out of court. They knew nothing of the subject
in dispute, and were unable to decide upon the political consequences of La Salle's discoveries. The map
of the Academy is equally objectionable. It bears a
date twenty years *after* the year in which France
ceded Louisiana to Spain, and the opinion of the
Academy upon it is of no more importance than that
of Mr Pople, the English map-maker. If such
authorities are in any case to be of any avail, the boundaries of the new republic of Texas could not admit
of dispute. Every late map published either in
America or in England, extend them so as to include
New Mexico, though that part of the country never
formed a portion of the department of Texas when
under the government of Mexico—though the people
of New Mexico have never recognised the government of Texas, and notwithstanding the fact, that
the government of the United States has always negotiated with that of Mexico, and not with the government of Texas, respecting its trade with Santa Fé,
even since its recognition of the independence of
Texas. The Spanish map, having no official authority,
must be rejected with the rest.

The only authorities produced on the part of the
United States, of the slightest value, were the work
of Joutel, the letter of La Harpe, and the order of
Bienville. Whatever claim was asserted could only
be inferred from the facts contained in them, and the

extent of any inference to be drawn from them will be shown presently.

On the part of Spain the argument was grossly misconducted. De Onis neither knew the case he was commissioned to support, nor was competent to use the few facts with which he was acquainted. He consequently sacrificed the interests entrusted to him.*

The object of La Salle's expedition to the Mississippi was to facilitate an aggression on the Spanish colonies. His landing in Texas was purely accidental ; but as soon as it was known, the few persons left by La Salle were captured by the Spaniards. Charlevoix, a French authority, recorded their fate : some of them were sent to the mines, and there

---

* Mr Greenhow states (p. 317) that De Onis published a defence of his negotiation, on his return to Spain in 1820, and that " he clearly shows that he was by no means convinced, that the territory in dispute, beyond the Sabine, did not properly form part of Louisiana ;" and that he expressly declares, that " his principal object in the long correspondence which he kept up on the subject was to gain time." If this is so, De Onis was as faithless to the rights of Spain, as he proved himself to be ignorant and incompetent in the protection of them.

The book of Mr Greenhow, to which frequent reference will be made in the following pages, is entitled " The History of Oregon and California, and the other Territories on the Northwest coast of North America. Boston, 1844." It is the extension of a memoir published by him in 1840, by the direction of the Senate of the United States, and therefore has an official character.

is no evidence that the French government ever demanded their release, or that any remonstrance was made respecting their treatment. An expedition, formed at Coahuila, under the command of Alonzo, de Leon, was directed to scour the country, and to hunt out the French, if there were any still remaining. He arrived on the 22nd of April, 1689, at a place where La Salle had built Fort St Louis, and on the 24th, at the entrance of the bay, where he found the remains of a French vessel that had been wrecked. On the 22nd of May of the same year, he wrote to the Viceroy to inform him that there were neither French nor any other foreigners in the whole country. (' Correspondence,' p. 32.)

The measures of France, which were intended to be hostile, were treated as hostile by Spain the moment they were known. The Spaniards had a perfect right thus to regard them. Before La Salle arrived they had discovered and settled on the Rio Grande. They had explored its southern course, and they had even made a settlement on its most northern banks in New Mexico. In the Archives of Sante Fé is a memorial of Don Juan de Oñate, a citizen of Zacatecas, dated September 21, 1595, asking permission to establish a colony on the Rio del Norte, and it appears by it, that even a previous settlement had been made in New Mexico by Don Francisco de Leyva Bonillo. The settlement then made does not appear to have been discontinued, and the journal of

Don Antonio de Oterman, who was governor and commandant there in 1680, was lately existing in the Archives of Sante Fé.—(Gregg's 'Commerce of the Prairies,' vol. i, p. 117—122.) How then can it be contended, in opposition to the fact of these settlements, which gave actual possession to Spain of the country on both banks of this great river, an hundred years before La Salle had even discovered the Mississippi, that his landing in Texas entitled France to territory extending to that river?

The government of Spain, however, not satisfied with its measures to scour the country of French intruders, instantly took active steps to establish a military occupation of it. In 1698 the Presidio of San Antonio de Bexar was built, and in 1716 that of Espiritu Santo, subsequently called Goliad. To the territory watered by the Guadaloupe, and to all west of it, Spain thus obtained an undisputed right, both by occupation and discovery, for La Salle never went west of the Colorado river. To the territory east of the Colorado, to which alone, on account of La Salle's discoveries, could any French claim be possibly set up, it made its title perfect by the destruction in the first instance of La Salle's fort on the Vaches, built only for a temporary purpose, by the establishment of the Presidio of St Miguel de los Adeas, existing in 1718, and by the establishment of the town of Nacogdoches in 1732. It had thus complete and entire possession of the country.

In the month of July, 1719, a dispute took place between La Harpe, a French officer, and Alarconne, a Spaniard, respecting the post of Nassonnite, on the eastern frontier of Texas; and on August 10, 1721, La Harpe was directed by Bienville, the Governor of Louisiana, to proceed with twenty soldiers, under the command of M. de la Belisle, to take possession of the Bay of San Bernard.—(' Correspondence,' Appendix.) But the acts of La Harpe and of Bienville do not appear to have received support from the French government. Spain, therefore, was in actual possession of Texas from the year 1786 at least, and it continued its possession when it acquired Louisiana in 1762. Previous to this acquisition it was a Spanish possesssion, and, therefore, as a Spanish possession undisturbed by any French title, it remained to the year 1819, when the negotiation with the United States took place. A title running over nearly 140 years existed, not shaken by any war, not disturbed by hostile incursions, and not the subject of official remonstrance with the imperial government of France, though for an instant questioned by colonial agents. There is not a single document of the French government to sustain the pretended authority of mere mapmakers. Against such facts as these, even if La Salle had made an actual settlement—if for years it had been successful, and Spain had subsequently ejected the settlers and occupied the country for above a century— its right to the country against France would have been established by every known and admitted principle upon which territorial claims are determined.

The negotiations between Spain and the United States were terminated by the treaty, called the Florida Treaty, signed at Washington on the 22nd of February, 1819. The claims of the United States to Texas were abandoned, but the Floridas were resigned to it by Spain. The Chevalier de Onis is said to have claimed " the praise of his nation for having *exchanged* the small and comparatively unimportant province of Florida for the rich and productive territory of Texas."—(Greenhow, p. 317, note.) But a more gross case of mismanaged and ignorant diplomacy was never exhibited, and it is not surprising that the ratification of the treaty was withheld by the Spanish government for nearly two years.

The south-western boundary of Louisiana previous to this treaty was the Arroyo, midway between Nachitoches and the Adeas, this having been the dividing line before the cession of Louisiana to Spain in 1762. By the Florida treaty the boundary west was fixed to be the river Sabine to the thirty-second degree of latitude, thence due north to the Rio Roxo or the Red River of Nachitoches, thence westward along this river to the degree longitude 100 west from London (*quære*, Greenwich) and 23 from Washington; thence due north to the river Arkansas; thence to its source in 42° latitude, or if the source is north or south of latitude 42°, along a line due north or south until it meets the parallel of latitude 42°; and thence along this parallel to the Pacific.

Thus was the undefined line (ante p. 37) from the Rocky Mountains to the Pacific inserted in the treaty with France converted into a defined line.

A sweeping clause was included in the treaty by which the United States ceded to Spain and " renounced for ever " all rights, claims, and pretensions to territories lying west and south of the described boundary, and Spain ceded to the United States all rights, claims, and pretensions to territories east and north of this boundary. This clause is the foundation of the claim of the United States to the Oregon territory, and will be noticed again hereafter.

The reason for abandoning the claims to Texas made by the United States was the acquisition of the Floridas. " For territory ceded by Spain, other territory of great value (Texas), to which our claim was believed to be well founded, was ceded by the United States, and in a quarter more interesting to her."—(' Message of President Munroe,' December 7, 1919.) Upon the establishment, however, of the independence of Mexico, proposals were made to change the limits fixed by the treaty. In 1825, during the presidency of Mr Adams, who had negotiated the Florida treaty, Mr Clay directed Mr Poinsett, the American minister in Mexico, to endeavour to negotiate a new boundary, " the line of the Sabine approaching nearer to the western coast than could be wished, and adding that the Mexican government might not be unwilling to adopt that of the Rio Brazos del Dios, or the Rio Colorado, or the Snow Mountains, or the Rio del Norte." In March 15, 1827, Mr Clay, finding probably that there was no willingness on the part of Mexico to make a donation of the desired acquisition, informed Mr Poinsett that the boundary to be preferred would be a line ascending the Rio del Norte to the Puerco, and thence along the Puerco to its source, and thence to the parallel 42°, and along this parallel to the sea; or if this could not be obtained, a line ascending the Rio Colorado. For the first, which included the whole of Texas, Mr Poinsett was authorised to offer one million of dollars, and for the second 500,000 dollars.

Mr Clay left office without having been able to obtain the concession he asked for.

On the 25th of August, 1829, Mr Van Buren instructed Mr Poinsett to endeavour to obtain a boundary line beginning at the Gulf of Mexico, in the centre of the desert, or grand prairie, west of the Nueces, and running north to the mountains, between the waters of the Rio Grande and the waters on the east, until it reached the 42° lat., or if this was not obtainable, any of the following, the one furthest west eing preferred—namely, secondly, a line from the mouth of the De la Baca, in Matagorda Bay, to its most westerly point, thence due north to the Colorado river, and thence by a line including the head waters

c

of the Arkansas and Red River, to the 42nd degree; or thirdly, a line running up the Colorado, and from its head waters to the 42nd degree; or lastly, a line running up the Rio Brazos del Dios, to the head waters of its most westerly branch to the point before indicated. "The President (General Jackson), it was added, did not desire the proposed cession without rendering a just and fair equivalent for it. He, therefore, authorises the offer to the Mexican government, for the cession of the first-mentioned boundary, of a sum not exceeding four millions of dollars, but so strong were his convictions of its great value to the United States, that he would not object, if it should be indispensably necessary, to go as high as five millions; but the interests of the United States were to be consulted by obtaining the cession upon terms as favourable, and for a price as low as possible."

Subsequently it was thought that a more extended boundary was desirable, and Mr Butler was informed by Mr Forsyth, that the President had been informed "that the Port of San Francisco, on the western coast, would be a most desirable place of resort for American vessels, and had directed an addition to be made to the instruction, relative to the negotiation for Texas, the main object of which should be to secure the whole Bay of San Francisco." The line to be proposed was to run up the Rio Brazos, north, to the 37th parallel of latitude, and thence along this parallel to the sea.

All these offers were, however, disposed of by the conduct of the Mexican Chamber of Deputies, in 1828, who appear to have distrusted their own government. They resolved that they would not take into consideration the treaty of commerce made with the United States, until an article should be inserted in it recognising the validity of the treaty made between Spain and the United States, in 1819. Mr Poinsett, in announcing this fact to his government, stated that, in reply to his proposals to alter the limits, it was insisted that Mexico had a right to consider this treaty binding on the United States, as being invested with all the rights of Spain, and bound by all the obligations of the mother country, and, he added, that the cession had been mentioned, made by Spain to Great Britain, of certain rights in the Bay of Honduras, which, however inconvenient to the Mexican government, it had nevertheless felt itself bound to ratify.

The United States, therefore, solemnly renounced all title to Texas by its treaty with Spain ; it accepted the Floridas on account of this renunciation; it offered a million of dollars to Mexico for the purchase of it, and it subsequently increased its offer to six millions. After this, it was not without surprise that the announcement of President Tyler, made to the Senate of the United States, on April 22, 1844, was heard :—

That he had negotiated with Texas a treaty for the annexation of the country to the United States, and that if it should meet with the approval of the Senate, "the government will have succeeded in *reclaiming* a territory which formerly constituted a portion, as is confidently believed, of its domain, under the treaty of cession of 1803 by France to the United States."

This reason at least ought to have been suppressed. It was one that in the heat of a debate would scarcely have been excusable, and it was not creditable to a person occupying the highest position in the country, and charged with the duty of sustaining its public engagements.

It is not, however, surprising, that in the United States a strong feeling should prevail to protect Texas in its present contest with Mexico. The independence of Texas was not the result of fraud, or a policy instigated by the government of the United States. Those of American origin, who first entered the country as colonists, between the years 1821 and 1835, did so under the guarantee of the Mexican government. They accepted a constitution, which made Texas, in conjunction with Coahuila, an independent State, and part of the Mexican confederation. They lived under Mexican laws, and certainly did not violate their engagements. But revolution after revolution took place in the city of Mexico, in which they had no share, and in which they did not even indirectly concur. Their laws were subverted, their political institutions set aside, and illegal demands were made upon them. They were forced to revolt for their own protection, and after having contended against a barbarous and sanguinary war, at last established their independence in the battle of San Jacintho, on the 21st of April, 1836. From this time until the present, the population of Texas has greatly increased; courts of law have been established throughout the country, and not the slightest wish has existed to disturb the new government. Four elections of Presidents have taken place without any disorder, and three Presidents have served their full term of office. Perfect security exists in every settlement, and the only danger apprehended by travellers is an occasional incursion of hostile Indians.

If the government of Texas has not always acted wisely, and has mismanaged its finances, its history since its independence most certainly presents a very favourable contrast to that of the government of Mexico. Where beyond the Rio Grande are the roads safe to travellers? Who that has visited the city of Mexico has failed to see murdered men almost daily exposed in the Acordada? And who will allege that the law has any influence in the country? On every side there is nothing but decay; the mineral and agricultural resources of the country neglected, and its foreign trade and commerce vexed by mischievous exactions. There are men in the country of great intelligence and ability, and the elements to sustain a good government exist, but a mighty military establishment overrides all, and exists

only to gratify the ambition of military chieftains.
Each revolution has been the result of a military, and
not of a popular, conspiracy. One President alone,
General Victoria, who was elected on the removal of
the Emperor Iturbe, has served the legal term of
office. In 1828 Pedraza was elected President, but
Guerrero was proclaimed by Santa Anna. In 1828
Pedraza retired, and in 1829 Guerrero became President. In 1831 Guerrero was shot, and Bustamente
was made President. In 1833 Pedraza was restored,
and on the same year Santa Anna became President.
In April, 1836, Santa Anna was taken prisoner by the
Texans, and Bustamente was again placed at the
head of the Republic. The revolution of 1841
drove Bustamente from the country, and Santa Anna
assumed the office he had lost by his imprison-
ment.

The resistance of the Texans to such a system of
change is perfectly justifiable, and their chief justifica-
tion is the peace they have enjoyed, while Mexico has
been convulsed by its civil dissensions. The law
has infinitively more respect paid to it by the
English population of America than is assumed
in this country, and each man is too intent upon
the promotion of his own interests, and under-
stands them too well to entertain any desire to
overthrow the government. But the evils of the
changes made in Mexico were felt by the friends and
relatives of the settlers throughout the Union, and the

government of the United States would have seriously experienced their injurious consequences, if they had not been checked by the establishment of the independence of Texas.

The conquest of Texas by Mexico cannot be accomplished. What would be the object of the attempt? If Mexico occupied the country, under what law would the people live? Under which of the many constitutions promulgated in Mexico? If they were to be deprived of the right of voting for public offices, and of the privileges of self-government, the scenes in Mexico itself would be re-enacted in Texas, and revolutions and civil contests would take place most injurious to the neighbouring States of America. If the conquest of the country means, what Santa Anna means it to be, namely, that every settler in it shall be driven out, then it should be remembered that they, nearly all of them, hold their lands under Mexican titles, and would contend to the last for their possession, and that such a conquest must, professedly, be a war of extermination. Are the people of America expected to witness this and not to interfere? And if, again, a Mexican army so far succeeded as to sweep over the whole country, yet Mexico could not continue its occupation. It has not the pecuniary means to maintain such an army, and above an hundred miles of desert lies between the Rio Grande and San Antonio. If posts were to be established, they would most certainly be captured in detail.

To prevent, then, an unnecessary war, which could not but disturb its own peace, and would fail in its object, the interference of the United States would be perfectly excusable.* But the President Munroe (Message, December 2, 1823) claimed a right to interfere in similar cases on another ground,—" with

---

* When the annexation of Texas was first proposed in the United States, General Santa Anna, after his return to Mexico, addressed a letter to General Houston, the President of Texas, dated November 5, 1836, expressing this opinion :—" The convention agreed upon on the 14th of May had for its fundamental principle that Texas should form an independent nation, and that it should enjoy a legal existence through the recognition of Mexico. This has been changed by the declaration which the people of Texas have made to unite themselves to the United States of the north—a fact which will reduce the question to a simple point (*sencilla*). The moment this pretension is admitted it will become necessary for the Cabinet of Washington to direct the negotiation, in which Mexico will not refuse to enter into the necessary explanations, and into such a definitive convention as may be desired. To avoid loss of time, and with a view to attain so important an object, and in order to conciliate, at the same time, all interests, is the object of my proposed conference with the Cabinet of Washington. Convinced as I am that Texas will not again re-unite itself with Mexico, I wish my country to derive all the advantages it can obtain, and to avoid the sacrifices it may incur in rashly endeavouring to re-conquer a country through which it has been more injured than benefited. It is thus that the Texan question can be reduced to the simple point of a settlement of the boundaries between the United States and Mexico which has been pending many years, and which may be fixed either at the River Nueces, or the Rio Bravo del Norte, or by some other line."

the governments which have declared their independence and maintained it, and whose independence we
have, on just principles, acknowledged, we cannot
view any interposition for the purpose of oppressing
them or controlling in any manner their destiny [by
any European power—namely, Spain] in any other
light than the manifestation of an unfriendly disposition towards the United States."

But how infinitely more important is the principle
of declaring that warfare shall not be a mere amuse-
ment—to be hopelessly carried on, when the peace of
neighbouring states is affected by it. If Mexico cannot understand the interests of Texas or establish a just
government in a colony, it cannot condemn an interference to sustain the independence which such colony
has obtained when other countries have recognised it for
the protection of their own interests. But the government of the United States has not on this occasion
claimed to interfere on this ground, nor on that set
forth by President Munroe. A certain party in office
has sought for the annexation of Texas, and at the
same time has declared that Mexico has a right to
attempt to conquer it. The meaning of which seems
to be, that the circumstances which might compel the
government of the United States to interfere for the
purpose of keeping its own frontier in subjection, shall
be converted into reasons to excuse the permanent
occupation of the country.

At present the annexation of Texas would not be

assented to by the necessary majority of American States. As long as its independence is secure, such a vote will not be given. But the character of Mexican warfare is such that the present state of opinion is not to be relied on. In Texas, also, the wish of the people is certainly to continue independent. Whatever vote indicating the contrary has been or may be given, will be occasioned by the necessity of its obtaining external aid.

Great Britain most properly refrained from recognising the independence of the country until there had been a long intermission of active hostilities on the part of Mexico. When it did recognise it, independent treaties had been made between it and the United States and France. The time had arrived when the measure could not be delayed. Since then, whatever may be the assertions of the American press to the contrary, it has acted in good faith ; it has neither instigated attacks on it, nor can the open and publicly declared wish that the institution of slavery should be modified under its laws be a just cause of complaint. It has not the social and political reasons of the United States to justify an active interference in the pending hostilities, though its commercial interests may render the interposition of its authority prudent.

But whether Texas remains independent or is annexed to the United States—and one of these two events is certain—it requires no spirit of prophecy to foretel that the Rio Grande north of Paso del Norte will not permanently be its north-western boundary.

II. On the Western or Oregon Boundary of the United States.

The first notice of the western boundary of Louisiana of any authority is in the grant of September 17, 1712, made by Louis XIV to Crozat. This grant empowered him " to carry on exclusively the trade in all our territories by us possessed and bounded by New Mexico, and by those of the English in Carolina; all the establishments, ports, harbours, rivers, and especially the port and harbour of Dauphin island, formerly called Massacre Island; the river St Louis, formerly called the Mississippi, from the sea-shore to the Illinois; together with the river St Philip, formerly called the Missouri river, and the St Jerome, formerly called the Wabash (the Ohio), with all the countries, territories, lakes inland, and the rivers emptying directly or indirectly into that part of the river St Louis. All the said territories, countries, streams, and islands, we will to be and remain comprised under the name of 'THE GOVERN- MENT OF LOUISIANA,' *which shall be dependent on the general government of New France, and remain sub- ordinate to it;* and we will, moreover, that all the territories which we possess on this side of the Illinois be united, as far as need be, to the general government of New France, and form a part thereof, reserving to ourselves to increase, if we think proper, the extent of the government of the said country of LOUISIANA."

This document defined with tolerable precision the province of Louisiana. It was partly bounded on the west by New Mexico; it was to reach the Illinois to the north, and it did not extend beyond the Rocky Mountains. It was also declared that the government should be dependent on the general government of New France —that was, subject to the superior authority of the governor of Canada. Some years subsequently the Illinois was added to Louisiana. On the west the province did not extend beyond the mountains. New Mexico bounded it, at least as high as 41 degrees, or above the source of the Rio del Norte. There was no strip of land to the west belonging to France, as mentioned in the treaty of 1803, "lying between the territory claimed by Great Britain on the one side and Spain on the other;" and Mr Greenhow admits " that we are forced to regard the boundaries indicated by nature—namely, the highlands separating the waters of the Mississippi from those flowing into the Pacific or the Californian Gulf—as the true western boundaries of Louisiana, ceded to the United States by France in 1803."—(Greenhow, p. 283).

The consequence, therefore, is, that the purchase of Louisiana included so much territory as was bounded on the north by a line running from the source of the Mississippi due west to the mountains, as will be shown presently; on the west by the mountains; on the east by the river Mississippi, and on the south by the Gulf of Mexico.

A still more important consequence is, that the title to the territory claimed by the United States, west of the mountains, dates from the year 1819, and is derivable from the Florida treaty made with Spain, and not from the treaty for the purchase of Louisiana made with France. The treaty with France in 1803, professed to give "a line" across some country lying between the territory claimed by Spain and Great Britain. The Florida treaty, which was made between Spain and the United States in order to carry into execution that made between France and the United States, defined the northern boundary of Mexico to be a line running along the forty-second parallel of latitude, from the mountains to the Pacific, and accompanied it with a cession of Spanish rights to the north. On the conclusion of this treaty, it was contended, on the part of the United States, that Great Britain had no title to any territory north of that parallel, on the ground that no other country but Spain had a right to such territory. It is, consequently, material to ascertain what were the English claims to the Oregon Territory prior to the year 1819.

The government of Spain during its possession of Mexico never made any settlement on the western coast north of Cape Mendocino (lat. 40° 29' N). It was a vacant territory, subject to the same rules of settlement that had governed the settlement of other portions of North America. "Having touched only here and there upon a coast," said Queen Elizabeth to the Spanish Ambassador, "and given names to a few rivers or capes, were such insignificant things as could in no ways entitle them (the Spaniards) to a propriety farther than in the parts where they actually settled and continued to inhabit." And the principle embodied in this speech has been the rule acted on by nearly every European nation.

The first voyage along the western coast of America, which it is necessary to notice, is that made by Juan Perez in 1774. The last voyage previously made by the Spaniards on this coast occurred as far back as the year 1603. No official account of the expedition of Juan Perez has been published, but it has been inferred that he discovered *Nootka Sound*, though it is admitted, at the same time, that the discovery of this important harbour is by general consent assigned to Captain Cook; and that the government of Spain "has deprived itself of the means of establishing beyond question the claim of Perez to the discovery."— (Greenhow, p. 117.)

On the return of Perez another expedition was sent to the North Seas by the Spanish government. It consisted of two vessels, the ' Santiago,' commanded by Don Bruno Heceta; and the 'Sonora,' commanded by Don Juan Francisco de la Bodega y Quadra, who succeeded Ayala after the vessel sailed, and who had with him Maurelle as pilot. Soon after leaving the Isle de Dolores, north of the Columbia, the vessels parted company. Bodega proceeded north

beyond the fifty-sixth degree of latitude, and examined the coast now belonging to and possessed by
Russia. The ' Santiago ' returned, and on the 15th
of August, 1775, Heceta observed an opening in the
coast in lat. 46° 17', from which rushed a current so
strong as to prevent his entering. This fact convinced him of the existence of a river, and he placed
it on his chart, under the name of the Rio St Roc.—
(Greenhow, p. 120). This is the first notice of the
Columbia river.

In the year 1778 Captain Cook visited the west
coast of North America, to which Drake had given
the name of New Albion. On the 7th of March he
reached the coast in 44° of north latitude. He continued his exploration north, but passed the Columbia
river without observing it. He discovered Nootka
Sound among other places, and having reached the
land at the foot of Mount Elias (lat. 60° 18'), continued his course round the coast to the Aleutian
islands. This was the first voyage in which any
survey of the coast that can be relied on, or that even
deserves the name, was made.

In 1779 Spain became involved in a war with Great
Britain, and its flag did not again appear on the coast
north of Cape Mendocino until 1788.—(Greenhow,
p. 126.)

In 1789 the seizure was made of the 'Iphigenia,'
the ' Argonaut,' the ' North-West America,' and the
'Princess,' at Nootka, by the Spanish captain, Martinez. Meares, the Englishman chiefly concerned in

the adventure and trade in which they were engaged, may, and certainly seems to have misrepresented several facts connected with it ; and he may have demanded and obtained, as always happens in demands for indemnification, more than was actually lost; but Martinez certainly exceeded his authority, for he was specially instructed by the Viceroy of Mexico not to capture any British vessels on the north-west coast. The personal facts of the case are not of the slightest importance ; the only question dependent on it is, whether or not the English or any other foreign nation had a right to trade on the coast, or to make settlements upon it ?

Now it is a clear and admitted fact that Spain never made any settlement north of Cape Mendocino. The whole coast for upwards of twenty-five degrees north of this cape was waste, unsettled, and unoccupied. Throughout the whole distance there was no person authorized to execute authority on the part of Spain, or any other power, at any single point.

The right of making settlements under such circumstances as these has been argued by Mr Greenhow, and his argument is too important, upon account of its admissions, to omit. He says :—

" It should be observed with regard to the right of the Spanish government to take possession of Nootka, that before the 6th of May, 1789, when Martinez entered the sound with that object, no settlement, factory, or other establishment whatsoever, had been founded or attempted ; nor had any jurisdiction been exercised by the authorities or subjects of a civilized nation in any part of America bordering upon the

Pacific, between Port San Francisco, near the thirty-eighth degree of north latitude, and Prince William's Sound, near the sixtieth. The Spanish, the British, the Russians, and the French had, indeed, landed at many places on these coasts, where they had displayed flags, performed ceremonies, and erected monuments, by way of 'taking possession,' as it is termed, of the adjacent territories for their respective Sovereigns ; but such acts *are, and were then. yenerally considered as empty pageants,* securing no real rights to those by whom or in whose names they were performed. Nor does it appear that any portion of the above-mentioned territories had become the property of a foreigner, either by purchase, occupation, or any other title which can be regarded as valid.

" The right of exclusive sovereignty over these extensive regions was claimed by Spain in virtue of the papal concesssion in 1493 of the first discovery of the coast by Spanish subjects, and of the contiguity of the territories to the settled dominion of Spain. Of the validity of the title derived from the papal concession, it is needless in the present day to speak. That the Spaniards were the first discoverers of the west coasts of America, as far north as the fiftieth parallel of latitude, has been shown ; and the fact is, and ever has been, since the publication of Maurelle's ' Journal ' in 1781, as indisputable as that the Portuguese discovered the south coasts of Africa. The extent of the rights derived from discovery are, however, by no means clearly defined by writers on public law ; and the practice of nations has been so different in different cases, that it seems impossible to deduce any general rule from it. That a nation whose subjects or citizens had ascertained the existence of a country previously unknown, should have a better right than any other to make settlements in that country ; and, after such settlement, to own it, and to exercise sovereignty over it, is in every respect conformable with nature and justice ; but this principle is liable to innumerable difficulties in its application to particular cases. It is seldom easy to decide how far a discovery may have been such, in all respects, as should give this strongest right to settle, or to what

extent of country a title of sovereignty may have been acquired by a particular settlement. And even when the novelty,
or priority, or sufficiency of the discovery are admitted, the
right of prior occupation cannot surely be regarded as subsist-
ing for ever, to the exclusion of all other nations ; and the
claims of states occupying contiguous territories are always to
be taken into consideration.'—' The *exclusive* right [claim] of
occupation must be distinguished from an exclusive right
[claim] to sovereignty [*quære*, from an alleged prior title to
occupy], as no nation could be justified by virtue of the former
right [*quære*, the latter pretension], and without occupation or
the performance of acts indicating an intention to occupy, in
depriving others of the trade of extensive vacant sea coasts,
unless upon the ground that the exercise of such trade would
be injurious to its actual interests in those countries."

Notwithstanding the alleged difficulty of determining when a country which has no title to occupy
a vacant territory by reason of discovery may occupy
it as abandoned, the practice in such cases has been
tolerably uniform. Discovery alone, and an alleged
intention to occupy, certainly do not give a perfect
title, unless an actual occupation takes place. Nor
does the discovery of part of a great territory entitle
the first settlers to take the whole. For instance, the
continent of North America was first discovered by
the English under Cabot ; but the right, nevertheless,
of the French to settle on it was never questioned.
The southern part of the same continent was occupied by Spain, but the French, nevertheless, made the
contiguous settlement of Louisiana. Where there is
clear evidence of abandonment—where the discovery

is not followed by preparations to occupy, a settlement may be made in opposition to a title of discovery. Where, also, the territory can be separated by any natural and distinct boundary—whether that of distance from prior settlements, or the physical facts of mountains or deserts—a settlement can be made in opposition to any previously made.

But " a settlement " must be understood to mean the establishment of the laws or government of the persons making the settlement, with the consent and authority of the nation to which they belong. Without such an authority they are mere outcasts and vagabonds on a desert; they have no right to form a government of themselves. A colony of the mother country—that is, a body of settlers among whom the law of their country can be administered — can only be formed by the consent of their own government. Discoveries actually accompanied by occupation, without such consent, do not entitle the settlers to any of the rights of their own govenment, or to exercise any power even of the most inferior description, under the pretence of being a colony. A settler can only have the authority that is delegated to him, and without such a delegation he has no power. The settlement he may make may be subsequently recognized by his own government, but unless it is so recognized it does not become a dependency of the nation of the settler.

At the time the English were at Nootka, the coast

was perfectly abandoned by Spain; there was no Spanish settlement on it. It was open to any nation to make a settlement, or to recognize any that had been made by its subjects without authority.

When the news arrived in England of the seizure of the vessels by Martinez, the British government claimed the right of having indemnification made to their owners; it determined to recognize any settlement that had been made; and it expressed its intention to make settlements. On the 5th of May, 1790, a message of the Crown was delivered to Parliament, complaining " that no satisfaction was made or offered for the acts of seizure, and that a direct claim was asserted by the Court of Spain to the exclusive rights of sovereignty, navigation, and commerce in the territories, coasts, and seas in that part of the world." The message was received by Parliament with much approbation, and the necessary supplies were very liberally granted to enforce the claims made.

In the declaration of Spain, dated Aranjuez, June 4, 1790, signed by the Conde de Florida Blanca, it is said that, " although Spain may *not* have establishments or colonies planted upon the coasts or in the ports in dispute, it does not follow that such coast or port does not belong to her." The British government alleged " that English subjects had an indisputable right to the enjoyment of a free and uninterrupted navigation, commerce, and fishery, and to the possession of such establishments as they should form with the consent of the natives of the country, not previously *occupied* by any European nation."

On the part of Spain there was no declaration of an intention to occupy; and on the other side, there was no assertion of a right to occupy in case occupation was taken by an European power.

The dispute was terminated by the convention between Great Britain and Spain, signed at the Escurial, October 28, 1790. By the third article it was agreed that the respective subjects of the contracting parties should not be molested in navigating or carrying on their fisheries in the Pacific Ocean or in the South Seas, or in landing on the coasts of those seas, in places not already occupied, for the purpose of carrying on their commerce with the natives of the country, or of *making settlements* there." But this article was subject to the restriction that the government of Great Britain should prevent an illicit trade with the Spanish settlements, and that the British should not navigate or fish within ten leagues of the coast already occupied by Spain. And it was by the fifth article agreed, that as well in the places restored as " in all other parts of the north-western coasts of North America, or of the islands adjacent, situated to the north of the parts of the said coast already occupied by Spain, wherever the subjects of either of the two powers shall have made settlements since the month of April, 1789, or shall hereafter make any, the subjects of the other shall have free access."

This convention was an admission of the right of the British government to make settlements, and the right insisted on is not to be distinguished from that of Russia to its settlements on the north-west coast. The admission of this right was not granted as a licence, liable to be revoked or lost by a war—it was not made as a favor or concession. It is one of those agreements respecting territory, such, for instance, as the treaty of 1783 made between Great Britain and the United States, which a war does not revoke. The admission contained in the convention is of a principle to which the States of America, the colony of Canada, and the State of Louisiana owe their existence. No new doctrine was set up. An old-established rule was recognized, and a war would have been the result if it had continued to be contested.

Mr Adams, whose long and distinguished career in the highest offices of his country had made him familiar with these questions, was compelled to treat it as a definitive settlement of a general principle of national law (Greenhow, p. 341, n.). And the President Munroe, in his message of December 2, 1823, admitted that no new principle had been asserted in the claims of Russia, and of Great Britain, to settle on the coast, but that the occasion had been found proper for asserting that " *henceforth* the American continents were not to be considered as subjects for European colonization." A declaration against which the Courts both of Russia and of Great Britain protested.

The convention did not exclude Spain from making settlements if it should think fit, but on the part of Spain the right of Great Britain to make them was acknowledged, and the intention and right of making one at Nootka Sound was especially declared and allowed.

When the convention was communicated to Parliament, it became the subject of party discussion, as every communication to a popular assembly will be. The just and wisely arranged treaty lately made between Great Britain and the United States respecting the north-eastern boundary of the United States— a treaty which ought, beyond all others, to have been accepted with unanimous approval, being a most honourable and fair settlement of a most complex question, did not escape the bitter though fortunately impotent criticism of a party opposition. Such attacks, when great interests are at stake—when unanimity might be instructive and no principle is compromised—may be regretted, but the language of them is not to be adopted in the interpretation of the policy of those whose acts are condemned. Mr Fox, Lord Grey, and the Marquis of Lansdowne contended that by the convention of the Escurial, nothing had been gained and much surrendered. " If the English," said Lord Grey, "form a settlement on one hill, the Spaniards may erect a fort on another." The English ministers did not enter into an explanation. They had not demanded the supplies, which enabled them to put afloat a great

armament, in order to effect so absurd an arrangement
as that described by the opposition. Mr Pitt was too
sagacious to have committed the blunders imputed to
him. The instructions given to Captain Vancouver,
who was commissioned to sail to the north-west coast
of America, and to take possession of Nootka Sound,
and to ascertain what parts of the coast were unsettled, contained his interpretation of the convention,
and they certainly appear to have been drawn up in conformity with an agreement with the Spanish government. On the 4th of June, 1792, after the survey of
a considerable extent of coast, Captain Vancouver, at
Possession Sound, took possession, " with the usual
formalities, of all that part of New Albion from the
latitude 39° 20′ south, and long. 236° 26′ E. to the
entrance of the inlet of the sea said to be the supposed
Strait of Juan de Fuca, as also of all the coasts,
islands, &c., within the said strait and both its
shores."

On the 23rd of June Captain Vancouver met the
Spanish schooners, the ' Sutil' and the ' Mexicana,'
under the command of Galiano and Valdes. The
communications between the commanders were of the
most friendly character. At Nootka, Vancouver
met the ' Dedalus,' with instructions from the British government, and he was referred to a letter
brought by the same ship from the Count de Florida
Blanca, addressed to the commandant of the fort of
San Lorenzo at Nootka, ordering that officer, in
conformity with the first article of the convention, to

put his Britannic Majesty's commissioners in possession of the buildings and districts, or parcels of land
which had been occupied by the English in April,
1789, as well in the port of Nootka as in Port Cox,
situated about sixteen leagues further southward.

The correspondence between Vancouver and the
Spanish commandant, Quadra, differed respecting
the extent of cession to be made, and they agreed to
submit the matter to their respective governments.

This expedition of the ' Sutil' and the ' Mexicana,' was the last made by the Spanish government
with the object of discovery in the North Sea. After
this the Spaniards abandoned the coast in dispute,
and never attempted to form an establishment upon it.
—(Greenhow, p. 257.) The order for the abandonment of Nootka was not merely sent by the ' Dedalus,'
but was communicated to that most eminent Viceroy
of Mexico, the Count de Revillagigedo,—a name ever
to be honoured.—(Greenhow, p. 227, n.)

After having taken possession of Nootka, Vancouver proceeded on the survey of the coast. Having met
with the American vessel the ' Columbia,' commanded
by Gray, he was informed of the river noticed by
Heceta, into which Gray had entered and named after
his vessel. Broughton was sent to examine the river,
and passed the bar. His survey extended inland for
upwards of one hundred miles from where he anchored
his ship. " Previously to his departure he formally
took possession of the river and the country in its

D

vicinity in his Britannic Majesty's name, having every reason to believe that the subjects of no other civilized nation or state had ever entered the river before. In this opinion he was confirmed by Mr Gray's sketch, in which it does not appear that Mr Gray either saw or was ever within five leagues of its entrance." *

---

* The very bitter tone in which Mr Greenhow speaks of Captain Vancouver, and his complaint that Captain V. endeavoured to deprive Gray of the honour of having seen the Columbia river, is not justified by the facts. It appears by the log-book of the 'Columbia,' that Gray crossed the bar of the river on the 11th of May, 1792. At one o'clock he anchored. At noon of the 14th he weighed anchor—at four o'clock he had sailed upwards of 12 or 15 miles, and at half past four o'clock the ship took ground, when she was backed off and again anchored. On the 15th Gray dropped down the river, and the subsequent movements were to get the vessel out. On the 20th he got clear of the bar. The river he named the Columbia, and called one point of the entrance Adam's point, and the other Hancock's point.

Captain Vancouver states (vol. ii, p. 53), that Broughton had with him a chart made by Gray—that he got to an inlet which he supposed the chart to represent, and passed Adam's point. After a minute description of it he says, " This bay terminated the researches of Mr Gray, and to commemorate his discovery, it was named ' Gray's Bay.' " This certainly proves that there was no wish to avoid acknowledging Gray's merits. The inlet from the sea to the river runs about east and west, and in the chart of Vancouver " Gray's Bay " is placed east of Adam's point, and far inland. On the 24th of October (1792) Broughton left the ' Chatham ' in lat. 46° 17', having brought it as far within the bay as he thought safe, and as far as he had reason to suppose the ' Columbia' had been brought.—(Vancouver,

Recognizing the merit of Gray, and admitting the claim that he is the first person who noticed the river after Heceta, who placed it on his chart within one mile of its true position, — still no claim can be set up upon this account by the United States. The *discovery* of a river, after the coast adjoining it has been discovered, has no peculiar virtue to exclude rights connected with the discovery of the adjoining coast. Before Gray entered the river, the entire coast had been traced. The *possession* of a river may be followed with important inland rights ; but Gray neither

---

vol. ii, p. 56.) He then proceeded to survey in a boat, taking with him a week's provisions. He proceeded up the river until the 30th, and calculated the distance he went, and which he particularly describes, " from what he considered to be the entrance of the river, to be 84, and from the 'Chatham' 100 miles." That is, that the entrance of the river was 16 miles (upwards of five leagues) above where he left the ' Chatham,' and consequently above where Gray anchored. He therefore came to the conclusion that Gray did not see what he called and explained to be " the entrance," and this conclusion is sustained by the distance mentioned in Gray's own log-book.

Thus the statement of Broughton and that of Gray are perfectly consistent, and there is nothing in Vancouver's relation of the facts of the case to justify the charge " that he possessed good temper and good feelings, except with regard to citizens of the United States, against whom and their country he cherished the most bitter animosity." So far from this being so, he makes the fullest acknowledgment of Gray's services—he retained the name of "Adam's point " on his chart, and he adopted that of Gray's ship, the ' Columbia,' as the name of the river. The error that Mr Greenhow has made has arisen from his taking a single sentence without the context. The inlet may

discovered it for the first time, nor had authority to take possession of it. In the discovery he had been anticipated by Heccta; he had no power to take possession, for he was in a private ship, pursuing his private affairs; and the private acts of an American citizen in such matters are not more important than similar private acts of English subjects.

The "taking possession" of new countries by authorized official persons is not the idle ceremony Mr Greenhow represents it to be. By the law of England, the Crown possesses absolute authority to extend its sovereignty; it can send its diplomatist to treat for, its soldier to conquer, its sailor to settle new countries. This it can do independently of Parliament: no act of the ordinary legislature is needed to establish English law and authority in such countries.

---

be considered as part of the river, but Broughton was justified in thinking it to be an arm of the sea. He concealed nothing, and gave his reasons for distinguishing the entrance of the river from the entrance to the inlet, for which he had the practice and authority of navigators. So far from misrepresenting the facts, the very evidence of Gray's log-book, which is produced to contradict him, verifies his statement. The veracity of Van-couver can never be disputed. He was incapable of what Mr Greenhow assumes that he did. He exhibited even an anxious care to recognize the previous discovery of Gray, and no American who shall read the whole account—though he may say that the entrance to the river is the entrance to the inlet—can come to the conclusion that any fact has been misrepresented, or that there was any attempt to do injustice to Gray. If Broughton had not explained what he meant, there would have been reason to complain.

A power of legislation is absolutely vested in the Crown for these purposes, which it can execute through the officers it may name. It can, also, as is well known to all Americans, legislate for such settlements independently of Parliament, or it may delegate its own power of legislation. The charter of Rhode Island granted by Charles II, and under which that State was governed until 1842, is an illustration of such legislation, and of the delegation of such authority. The Crown in that case, by its own legislative act, established English laws in that colony, and delegated its power of legislation to a very popular local legislature.

The "taking possession," therefore, of a new country by persons officially authorized — and no private person can assume the authority—is the exercise of a sovereign power, a distinct act of legislation, by which the new territory becomes annexed to the dominions of the Crown.

These principles were lately insisted on by the government *against* British subjects:—

"Neither individuals," said Governor Sir George Gipps, in a most luminous and admirable argument (New Zealand papers, May 11, 1841, No. 311, p. 64), "nor bodies of men belonging to any nation, can form colonies except with the consent and under the direction and control of their own government; and from any settlement which they may form without the consent of their government they may be ousted. This is simply to say, that as far as Englishmen are concerned, colonies cannot be formed without the consent of the Crown."—"I thought a declaration of the nature of that which stands in the preamble necessary, upon the same grounds that it was thought necessary by the Committee of the House of Commons in 1837, and I think it is the more necessary now when I see the gross ignorance which prevails upon this subject, even among persons otherwise well informed,—when I hear persons, and even lawyers, contend that Englishmen may set up a government for themselves whenever they like, and regardless alike of the Queen's authority and their own allegiance. Why, Captain Cook had as much right to purchase New Zealand for himself when he discovered it, or I had as much right to purchase the island of Tongataboo from the chief of that country, who came to visit me the other day, as Mr Wentworth had to purchase the Middle Island of New Zealand from the savages who were in Sydney in February last. When I cast my eye over the vast Pacific, and the innumerable islands with which it is studded, and consider that one man may seize an island here and another an island there, and that by dint of making themselves troublesome they may in the end render the interference of the government necessary, it is time to let people know that the law of England does not admit of such practices."

The constitution of other countries vests a similar sovereign authority in the Crown to that existing in Great Britain; but under the American constitution the President has no authority of the kind; he cannot annex territories to existing States, nor by his own act enlarge the boundaries of American dominions. The constitution has, in its first article, vested " all legislative power " in Congress. Before, therefore, the sovereignty of the United States can be established in a new territory, there must be an equivalent act of legislation by Congress to that necessary to be performed by the English Crown. How otherwise is it to be known to what country the territory belongs ?

After a country has had a new territory formally annexed to it, there doubtless remain other acts to be performed to complete the title, such as actual settlement, &c.; or otherwise, the inference of other countries is that the intention to occupy is abandoned. But the prior right to settle continues, even if there is a ground to imagine an intention to abandon, until some other country shall actually, and according to the forms which its laws sanction, establish its own laws and authority in the country.

In 1805 Louis and Clarke, who had been commissioned in the previous year, by President Jefferson, to explore the country west of the Rocky Mountains, reached the Columbia river, and returned to the United States in 1806. But this act of exploration, not resting on an original right of discovery, nor accompanied by any act of American legislation respecting the country, nor by any attempt to occupy, clearly does not establish a title to the territory west of the mountains. Nor is such a title set up. " Politically, the expedition was an announcement to the world of the intention of the American government to occupy and settle the countries explored." — (Greenhow, p. 288.) But such intention had already been announced to the world by the English government in a far more public, authentic, and legal manner, and its sovereignty over the country declared.

In 1810 Captain Smith, from Boston, built a house and garden on the south bank of the Columbia, but abandoned it before the close of the year. This was the act of a private person, and no political inference can be drawn from it.

In the same year Jacob Astor, of New York, formed the "Pacific Fur Company." He communicated his intention to the British North-West Company, and offered to it one-third of the interest of the scheme. The proposal was not accepted, and it is asked "if Mr Astor, a citizen of the United States, was justifiable in thus offering to an association of British subjects, noted for its enmity to his adopted country, a share of the advantages to be obtained under the flag of the United States, from territories exclusively belonging to the United States, and of which the exclusive possession by the United States was evidently essential to the advantage and welfare of the republic?"—(Greenhow, p. 294.) An English subject would have been free to make such an offer. Exclusive possession of the country by the United States certainly did not exist, for it had not taken any step either to claim, to possess it, or to annex it. When the company was formed, "the majority not only of the inferior servants, but also of the *partners*, were British subjects."— (Greenhow, p. 295.) They made an establishment on the Columbia river, but in consequence of difficulties, Macdougall and Mackenzie announced their determination, on the 1st of July, 1812, to dissolve the company, and Mr Hunt, another of the partners, in

August, 1813, acceded to it. On the 16th of October, 1813, an agreement was made between Messrs Mactavish and Alexander Stuart, on the part of the British North-West Company, and Messrs Macdougall, Mackenzie, and Clarke, on the other part, by which all the establishments, furs, stock in hand, of the Pacific Company, in the country of Columbia, were sold to the North-West Company for about 58,000 dollars. The difficulties which caused this dissolution might, it is said, have been overcome, " if the directing partners on the Columbia had been Americans instead of being, as the greater part were, men unconnected with the United States by birth, or citizenship, or previous residence, or family ties."— (Greenhow, p. 305.) It was, therefore, a settlement made by a majority of English, and the sovereignty of the English government having been declared over the country, they were amenable to English laws. Mr Astor could not annex the territory to the United States, and his sole object was to obtain furs. Shortly after the sale was made, a British sloop of war, the ' Racoon,' reached the Columbia, and the name of Fort George was given to the establishment.

Supposing, however, that the war between Great Britain and the United States had not broken out about this time, and that the ' Racoon ' had brought to Columbia, a judge, or a commission to any of the partners, to act as judge in the civil and criminal affairs of the colony, could the United States, or any other country, have insisted that he could not have exercised jurisdiction ? Could any persons who were there have exempted themselves from the jurisdiction of such a court? But, on the other hand, let it be supposed that the President of the United States had sent a commission to any person to administer the law there; would that commission have been operative? Would the Supreme Court of the United States have held, that in countries over which the legislature of the United States has not established its law,—which had not been annexed to or possessed by its government, that the President could deal with men's lives, with their fortunes, and property, or govern beyond the jurisdiction of American law?

The United States had not subjected the Oregon or the Columbia to its authority. It formed no part of any existing State; it was not a portion of a territory over which it had legislated, or even claimed to legislate.

The British government, on the contrary, had declared its intention to establish its law there, and it had attached it to its dominions in a formal and authentic manner. When the North-West Company took possession of the establishment in 1813, an authorized colony of British subjects from that moment was formed, subject to and governed by English laws—an actual occupation of the country was made, and a settlement on the river has continued until the present day. A more perfect title could not be proved.

At the termination of the war between Great Britain and America, a demand was made for the restoration of the post sold by Mr Astor's partners, as a portion of the territory of the United States taken during the war. The answer was, that it had not been captured; that the Americans had retired from it under an agreement of sale; that the North-West Company had purchased it; that the territory had early been taken possession of in his Majesty's name, as it had been by Broughton in Vancouver's expedition, and that it had been since considered to form a part of his Majesty's dominions.—(Greenhow, p. 307.) It was, however, agreed that the post should be restored, and "that the question of the title to the territory should be discussed in the negotiation as to limits and other matters, which was soon to be commenced."*

In 1819 Spain ceded to the United States its rights north of the parallel of latitude.

The British government, in its negotiation respect-

---

* I cite this statement in the words of Mr Greenhow (p. 308), because in subsequent pages, which he heads 'British Views of National Faith' (310, 312), he declares that Fort George was delivered up without any reservation or exception, and expresses his disbelief that Sir Charles Bagot, the British minister, communicated to the American government, in pursuance of Lord Castlereagh's direction of the 4th of February, 1818, the fact that Great Britain claimed the territory, and insisted that the American settlement was an encroachment. The delivery was clearly the execution of the conditional agreement mentioned in the text.

ing the Oregon boundary, has offered to the United States to fix the limits of part of their respective possessions by a line drawn down the Columbia River to the sea, and not to insist on the exclusive possession of it. It is, therefore, needless to inquire what might have been the extent of English claims, though in the negotiation of 1819 Mr J. Q. Adams informed the Chevalier De Onis that the following principles, which are applicable to this case, were asserted by the American government.—(' Correspondence,' p. 89.) :—

" First, that when any European nation takes possession of *any extent of sea coast*, that possession is understood as extending into the interior country to the sources of the rivers emptying within that coast—to all their branches, and the countries they cover ; and to give it a right in exclusion of all other nations to the same.

"Secondly, that whenever one European nation makes a discovery, and takes possession of any portion of this continent, and another afterwards does the same at any distance from it, where the boundary is not determined by the principles above mentioned, that the middle distance becomes such course.

" Thirdly, that whenever any European nation has thus acquired a right to any portion of territory on this continent, that right can never be diminished or affected by any power by virtue of purchases made by grants or conquests of the natives within the limits thereof."

It will be most convenient to notice the limits temporarily agreed on affecting the Oregon territory, when noticing the north-western boundary. But from the facts mentioned, it may be concluded that Spain never occupied, but abandoned the west coast of North America; that the British government announced its intention to occupy, and formally declared the annexation of parts of the coast to its own territory, acting in this respect as the government of Russia has done; and that the British settlement on the Columbia was the first of a national and legal character recognizable as such by foreign nations.

III. On the North and North-western Boundary of the United States.

"Louisiana, it is said, stretched from the Gulf of Mexico to the northward, and north-westward to an undefined extent."—(Greenhow, p. 276.)

It can be most distinctly demonstrated that there is not the slightest foundation for this statement.

Before the settlers who accompanied La Salle sailed to establish the colony of Louisiana, Beaujeau promised to act under the orders of the Governor and Intendant of Canada—(Ante p. 16).

In the grant made by Louis XIV to Crozat, it is distinctly mentioned that Louisiana was to be subordinate to the general government of New France (Canada). The extent of the province north was to be to the Illinois (ante p. 59)—but the Illinois was subsequently added to it.

So much as was not carved out of and added to Louisiana remained the province of Canada. The government of Canada had the control of the whole, and the jurisdiction of the subordinate could only be over the territory defined as the province of Louisiana. This province did not extend in 1712 further to the north than the Illinois, and the subsequent addition of the Illinois extended the province no further than the Illinois. All to the north remained part of Canada.

When France ceded Canada to England in 1762, it "ceded and guaranteed to Great Britain, in full right, Canada, with all its dependencies"—"and in general everything that depends on the said countries, lands, islands, and coasts, with the sovereignty, property, possession, and all rights acquired by treaty or otherwise, which the most Christian King and the Crown of France have had till now over the said countries, islands, places, coasts, and their inhabitants."

This concession was made with the distinct and defined purpose of including the whole district to the north and north-west of the source of the Mississippi. During the first negotiations, in 1761, for the cession of Canada, the limits between Louisiana and Canada were a subject of controversy. The desire of the English government was to extend the boundary of Canada over the Illinois, so as to reach the Mississippi through that country. This, also, was very early the expressed wish of those to whom the surrender of Canada was made; for the Marquis de Vandreuil, who signed the surrender, declared that ten days after it, he was asked for his maps, which he complained had been improperly taken from him, and that on being shown one by an officer, he pointed out errors:—" I told him the limits marked on it were not just, and verbally mentioned others extending Louisiana on the one side to the carrying place of the Miamis, and on the other to the head of the Illinois."—(' Annual Register,' 176, p. 267.) The highest point of Louisiana at the time of the surrender of Canada was the head waters of the Illinois.

But the question of the boundary between Canada and Louisiana was far too important to be left unsettled, and the English government would not assent to any qualified propositions respecting it. M. Bussy, on the part of France, endeavoured to make large exceptions in the cession of Canada, but Mr Pitt would not listen to them, as they included vast countries which Vandreuil had yielded under the description of Canada. Exceptions were then attempted to be made respecting the savage nations, but the English government insisted on the full and complete cession of the province. These negotiations failed; but in the following year not merely was an unconditional cession of Canada made in the words cited, but the Illinois was ceded, which was admittedly part of Louisiana.

First, then, as a subordinate province, partly formed out of Canada, Louisiana extended no further than the distinct boundaries of it could be shown; secondly, it never extended further north than the Illinois river; thirdly, the question of the extent of Louisiana was argued at the peace of 1762; fourthly, Canada in its full extent was ceded to Great Britain; and lastly, the official map used by France in its negotiations with Great Britain, incontestably proves that the country north and north-west of the Mississippi was ceded as the province of Canada.

No better authority for the above statement can be cited, than that M. Duflot de Mofras, a gentleman attached to the French legation at Mexico, and the author of a work on California, published by the order of the French government. To avoid the possibility of misinterpretation, his own words are cited:—

"Le traité de reconnaissance de l'indépendance des Etats-Unis, signé par l'Angleterre en 1782, ceux des 20 Janvier et 30 Septembre 1783, ainsi que les traités de 1794 et 1795 entre l'Angleterre et les Etats-Unis, ne font pas mention, à l'article, *frontières*, des territoires situés à l'ouest des Montagnes-Rocheuses. Le dernier seulement stipule que les possessions de la Compagnie d'Hudson ne seront pas accessibles aux citoyens des Etats-Unis. Or si les limites entre la Nouvelle-France et cette Compagnie n'ont pas été nettement déterminées, même après le traité d'Utrecht en 1713 et celui de la cession du Canada en 1763, il est incontestable que, ou la Nouvelle-France, ou les territoires de la Compagnie d'Hudson s'étendaient jusqu'à la mer Pacifique, et que si les Espagnols ont

reconnu les premiers la côte nord-ouest de l'Amérique, les Français, les premiers, ont découvert l'in-
térieur du continent en allant de l'est à l'ouest.
Toutes les anciennes cartes, en effet, d'accord avec les
auteurs les plus avérés, n'arrêtent qu'à la la mer du
Sud la limite des possessions françaises du Canada.
L'Escarbot, qui écrivait en 1617, entre autres, dit
textuellement : ' Ainsi nostre Nouvelle-France a pour
limites du côte d'ouest les terres jusqu'à la mer dite
Pacifique en deçà du tropique du cancer; au midi,
les isles de la mer Atlantique, du côté de Cube et de
l'isle Hespagnole; au Levant, la mer du Nord qui
baigne la Nouvelle-France, et au septentrion, cette
terre qui est dite inconnue, vers la mer glacée
jusqu'au pôle arctique.'

"Enfin, dans une carte gravée en 1757, et annexée
aux Mémoires des commissaires des Rois de France
et d'Angleterre en Amérique, on peut constater que
la Nouvelle-France s'étendait jusqu'à la mer Pacifique, et l'on y trouve, à la côte ouest de l'Amérique, sous le 46°, une grande rivière tracee dans une
direction exactement conforme à celle du Rio-Co-
lombia. Cette particularité n'a d'ailleurs rien qui
doive surprendre, puisqu'à partir de 1711 jusqu en
1754, les capitaines-généraux de la Nouvelle-France
dirigèrent de nombreuses expéditions au couchant du
Canada, et qu'après trente années d'incessantes ex-
plorations sous le gouvernement éclairé du Marquis
de Beauharnais, un officier, M. de la Vérendrye,

acquit une connaissance parfaite du fleuve et de la mer de l'Ouest, qui n'étaient autres que l'Océan Pacifique et la Colombie."*

By the 7th article of this cession, the line drawn from the source of the river Mississippi to the south, gave to Great Britain all the lands on the east bank of the river, and secured to France and through it to Spain, the territory west of the same line. But the territory of Canada, north of the source of the river (47° 10′ N. lat.), and north of a line running west of the source of the river, was left as part of Canada, of which it most indisputably formed a portion.

---

* On the general question, M. Duflot de Mofras, whose work on California exhibits no partiality towards the English, comes to the conclusion that the claims made by the Americans are without foundation :—

"Pour la limite du sud, le Mexique et l'Espagne ont agi de la même manière: ils ont concédé aux Etats-Unis leurs droits sur les contrées situées au nord du 42° parallèle ; mais il est de toute évidence qu le traité des Florides ne saurait porter atteinte à la validité de la convention de 1790, il ne constitue qu'une simple renonciation, et les Etats-Unis en y adhérant, s'étant substitués à l'Espagne pour le territoire à l'égard duquel cette puissance résignait ses prétentions, doivent respecter tous les droits qu'un traité antérieur au leur avait reconnu aux Anglais. Si nous avions maintenant à émettre une opinion sur cette question importante, nous ne pourrions, malgré nos sympathies pour les Etats-Unis et notre aversion contre le système d'envahissement de l'Angleterre, nous empêcher de reconnaître que la raison et le droit sont cette fois de son côté. Il est même permis de s'étonner que, répudiant sa ténacité habituelle, elle ait fait, aux Américains, dans le cours des négociations, de si larges sacrifice."

In the treaty made between Great Britain and the United States, nothing west of a line running north from the source of the Mississippi, to the line running due west of the furthermost point of the Lake of the Woods was granted to the United States (ante p. 36). All, therefore, north of a line running west, from the source of the Mississippi, that is, the country north of a parallel of latitude of about 47 degrees, was English territory, and a part of Canada, unconceded by any treaty, until the late convention of 1818.

The great lakes to the west and to the north-west of the source of the Mississippi had been discovered by the French, and formed part of Canada long previous to the cession of the province. Under the British government the exploration inland has continued, and in Mackenzie's expedition he crossed the continent and reached the sea. In different parts of this district, British forts, or posts, have been established, and, for its better government, the British Act of Parliament, of the 43 Geo. III. (A. D. 1803), gave additional powers to the Governor-General of Canada to facilitate the punishment of offences.

The extreme north-western part of the coast of North America forms a portion of Russian territory. The title to it is partly that of discovery, and partly that only of occupation. The chief establishments, if not the only ones, formed on it, were made subsequently to the year 1798, when the coast from the 55th degree of north latitude, northwards, was conceded to the Russian American Company. The Company was authorized to explore and bring under subjection to the Imperial Crown any other territories in America, not previously attached to the dominions of some civilized nation.—(Greenhow, p. 269). So that the Russian government, six years after the dispute respecting Nootka Sound, between Spain and Great Britain, acted on the principle admitted in the convention of the Escurial, and directed establishments to be formed on vacant and unsettled parts of the coasts.

In 1824, a convention was signed between the government of the United States and Russia, by the 3rd article of which it was agreed that the citizens of the United States should not form settlements to the north of 54° 40¹ of north latitude, and that the subjects of Russia should not form establishments to the south of that parallel. The principle upon which this convention proceeded cannot be distinguished from that on which the claim of the British to part of the coast is founded. But if the government of the United States anticipated the squeezing out of British claims by this union with Russia, it was checked by the convention made in 1825 between Great Britain and Russia, by which the boundaries of the Russian territory are very distinctly defined—and the intended effect of the convention with the United States, as far as the United States was interested in it—was checked.

In the assertion, then, of a strict right, the northern-western boundary should be a line commencing at the source of the Mississippi, and running west; and agreeably to the principles laid down by the American government (ante p. 84), it should include both banks of the Columbia. But in a treaty signed between the plenipotentiaries of Great Britain and the United States, in April, 1807, it was agreed that " a line drawn north or south (as the case might require) from the most north-western point of the Lake of Woods, until it shall intersect the 49th parallel of latitude, and from the point of such intersection due west, along and with the said parallel shall be the dividing line between his Majesty's territories and those of the United States, to the westward of the said lake, as far as their respective territories extend in that quarter—*provided* that nothing in the present article shall extend to the north-west coast of America, or to the territories belonging to or claimed by either party on the continent of America to the westward of the Stony Mountains." Unlooked-for events prevented the ratification of the treaty, and the subject was not again discussed until 1814.*

---

* The argument of Mr Greenhow (p. 281), that the reason for adopting the 49th parallel of latitude, namely, the treaty of Utrecht, and the acts of the commissioners, is founded on so manifest an error respecting the extent of Canada, that it does not merit discussion. The adoption of the 49th parallel was a just arrangement, to both Great Britain and the United States,

In 1818 a convention was ratified between Great Britain and America, after a long negotiation, in which the facts already related formed the basis, by which the rights of both countries were subjected to a temporary compromise. It was agreed that a line should be the northern boundary along the 49th parallel of latitude from the Lake of the Woods to the Rocky Mountains, and that the country westward of the Rocky Mountains should be free and open for the term of ten years from the date of the convention to the vessels, citizens, and subjects of both powers, without prejudice to the claims of either country.

At the end of ten years the negotiations on this subject were again renewed. It was proposed by Mr Canning and Mr Huskisson that the boundary beyond the Rocky Mountains should pass from those mountains westward along the 49th parallel of latitude to the north-easternmost branch of the Columbia river, and thence down the middle of the stream to the Pacific. This was not agreed to, and the negotiation terminated for a time.

On the 6th of August, 1827, a convention was signed, renewing the provisions of the former one of October 20, 1818, and extending it for an indefinite

---

though it gave less than the former had a title to insist on. Mr Jefferson was perfectly satisfied with it—but feared that the allusion to any claim extending to the coast would be offensive to Spain.—(Greenhow, p. 282). This was in 1807, after the purchase of Louisiana.

period, until either party should annul it, on giving a year's notice.

An argument was advanced in favour of the claim of the United States, on the ground of *contiguity*. But it is one of even more force, if it has any, in favour of Great Britain, than of the United States. It means, if anything, that part of the territory claimed is essential to the perfect enjoyment of the contiguous territory. Now the western trade of North America is chiefly that of peltries obtained by the English, and exported from Fort Vancouver, on the Columbia, and an access to the river is important to its continuance.

In the state above-mentioned, the question at this time remains. It is understood that negotiations are about to be or have been renewed for its settlement. They have been confided to Mr Pakenham, the British minister, who will not be directed to propose, nor would he ask, or demand, anything inconsistent with a just or a proper respect for American as well as British claims.

Hitherto, notwithstanding the remarks which have been made by American writers, the British government has acted with great temper and moderation. It has not placed its case on extreme right, and it has been actuated by a very sincere desire to maintain friendly relations with the United States. The errors of fact which have been committed in the course of the negotiations, have been upon very immaterial points, not in the slightest degree affecting the main question.

It is greatly to be lamented, however, that in America it should have been the interest of dishonest and violent politicians to have adopted a tone of discussion upon the subject opposed to its fair settlement. It is not honourable, while the title to the territory is undetermined between the respective governments, to urge measures to *populate* it with American citizens, in order to give facilities for its occupation at a future period. Such recommendations do not indicate a conviction of the validity of the claim insisted on. America, as well as Great Britain, has an interest in the establishment of a settled government in that part of the world—in marking out the limits of legal possession—and in rearing a population which, however they may differ respecting the system of government which they may prefer, shall look to the future, as bringing the fruits of a peaceful, generous, and civilized intercourse.

" MEMOIR OF M. CAVELIER DE LA SALLE ON
AN ENTERPRISE WHICH HE HAS PRO-
POSED TO MONSEIGNEUR THE MARQUIS
OF SEIGNELAY RESPECTING ONE OF THE
PROVINCES OF MEXICO."

MEMOIR, ETC.

The principal result which the Sieur de la Salle expected from the great perils and labours which he underwent in the discovery of the Mississippi, was to satisfy the wish expressed to him by the late Monseigneur Colbert, of finding a port where the French might establish themselves and harass the Spaniards in those regions from whence they derive all their wealth. The place which he proposes to fortify lies 60 leagues above the mouth of the River Colbert, (Mississippi) in the Gulf of Mexico, and possesses all the advantages for such a purpose which can be wished for, both upon account of its excellent position and the favourable disposition of the savages who live in that part of the country.

The right of the King to this territory is the common right of all nations to lands which they have discovered—a right which cannot be disputed after the possession already taken in the name of his Majesty, by the Sieur de la Salle, with the consent of the greater number of its inhabitants. A colony can easily be founded there as the land is very fertile and produces all articles of life—as the climate is very mild—as a port or two would make us masters of the whole of this continent—as the posts there are good, secure, and afford the means of attacking an enemy or of retreating in case of necessity—and also since all things are found there requisite for refitting. Its distance inland will prevent foreigners from sending fleets to attack it, since they would be exposed to destruction by fire which they could only avoid with difficulty in a narrow river, for if fire ships were sent down they would not fail to fall a-board them under the favour of night and of the current. The coast and the banks being overflowed for more than 20 leagues above the mouth, make it inaccessible by land, and the friendship of the savages towards the French, and the hatred which they bear toward the Spaniards, will serve also as a strong barrier.

These Indians, irritated by the tyranny of the Spaniards, carry on a cruel war against them, without even the aid of fire arms, which they have not yet had. On the other hand, they have been so conciliated by the gentleness of the Sieur la Salle, that they have made peace with him and offered to accompany him anywhere, and he has no doubt that they would favour his enterprise as much as they would oppose themselves to those of the enemies of France. This, any person may judge of by the offerings which were made at the posts on which the arms of France were attached, and by the assembly of more than

18,000 Indians of various nations, some of whom had come from a distance of more than 2,000 leagues, who met together in a single camp (*village*)—and who, forgetting their own old disputes, threw themselves into his arms and made him master of their different interests—and also from the deputations sent to him by the Cicaças and the Kansas, and other nations offering to follow wherever he might be pleased to lead them. By the union of these forces it would be possible to form an army of more than 15,000 savages, who, finding themselves supported by the French and by the Abenaki followers of the Sieur de la Salle, with the aid of the arms which he has given them, would not find any resistance in the province which he intends to attack, where there are not more than 400 native Spaniards, in a country* more than 150 leagues in length and 50 in breadth, all of whom are officers or artisans better able to explore the mines than to oppose themselves vigorously to an expedition which would moreover be favoured by Mulattoes, Indians, and by Negroes if their liberty were promised to them.

Upon account of these considerations the Sieur de la Salle proposes, with the approbation of Monseigneur, to undertake this enterprise, and if peace should

---

* This proves that the Spaniards were in the occupation of this part of the country at this time—a fact which has been denied.

prevent the execution of it, he offers to establish a very advantageous station for commercial purposes, very easy to be maintained, and from whence, at the commencement of hostilities, it would be possible to take from the Spaniards a good part of their mines.

New Biscay is the most northern province of Mexico, and is situated between 25° and 27° 30' of north latitude. It is bounded to the north by vast forests frequented by the people called Terliquiquimeki, whom the Spanish only know by the name of "*Indios Bravos y de guerra*," never having been able to subdue them, or to compel them to live in peace. From this province they extend themselves as far as the River Seignelai, which is distant from it in some parts 40 and in some 50 leagues. On the east it is bounded by the same forest, by the River Panuco, from which it is separated by a chain of mountains, which also form its limits to the south, from the province of Zacatecas to the west, from that of Culiacan to the north-west, where it separates the latter province from the new kingdom of Leon, not leaving more than two or three passages by which succours could be expected.

The distance from Mexico, which is more than 150 leagues, increases these difficulties, without speaking of the necessity which the viceroys would have of dividing their forces in order to defend the maritime districts, and the small number of native Spaniards to be met with in this vast extent of country, from whence no succours are to be obtained but with great loss of time and trouble—the height, also, of the mountains which they must pass for this purpose are too rough for a people enervated by long inactivity to be able to surmount without great means of conveyance and train. Even if succours could arrive more quickly than is presumed, the proximity of the woods and of the river would aid as much to secure a retreat and preserve any booty as it is favourable to an irruption of which the enemy would have no information before we should be in the middle of his territory.

As they do not think themselves to be in danger of being attacked, except by savages, they have no one place capable of sustaining an attack, though the country is very rich in silver mines, more than 30 having been already discovered. These would be much more profitable to the French on account of the proximity of the river, which would serve for the transport of the metals; whereas the Spaniards, from ignorance, from fear of the savages, and on account of the personal interest of the viceroys, transport the silver at a great expense as needless to us as it is to them inevitable at so great a distance.

Assuming, then, these facts, the Sieur de la Salle offers, if the war continues, to leave France with 200 men; 50 more will join him who are in the country, and 50 buccaneers (*flibustiers*) can be taken in passing St Domingo. The savages who are at Fort St Louis, to the number of more than 4,000 warriors, together with many others who will join, can be directed to descend the river. This army he will divide in three divisions, to maintain it more easily. In order to compel the Spaniards to divide their forces, two of these divisions shall each be composed of 50 French, 50 Abenakis, and 200 savages. They will receive orders to attack at the same time the two extremities of the province, and on the same day the centre of the country will be entered with the other division, and it is certain that we shall be seconded by all the unhappy in the country who groan in slavery. The English colony of Boston, although it is more powerful than all those of Spain, has been desolated by 600 savages. Chili has been ruined by the Araucanians, and the evil which the Iroquois, although without discipline or generalship, have done in Canada, are instances from which we may infer how disastrous is this mode of warfare to those who are not experienced in it, and also what may be expected from the aid of savages led by experienced Frenchmen having much knowledge of the country.

This province being taken, its approaches may be protected by Indians and mulattoes, who may be required to occupy the narrowest passes of the mountains, by which alone it can be entered, and fire arms may be given to them to defend it with greater efficiency. This undertaking is certain of success if it is executed in this manner, since the Spaniards cannot be prepared to defend passes of which they have no knowledge; whereas, if attacked by the River Panuco, or by sea, in open warfare, before the maritime places are conquered, or the River Panuco is ascended, which is populated from its mouth by their settlements, they would have leisure to occupy passes, with which they are well acquainted, and to make the result doubtful, or at least more difficult.

It is true that, in order to make a diversion, the buccaneers (*flibustiers*) might be of service if they were previously to make an attack and made descents on the coast, for then they would attract the Spanish troops to that side, who would thus leave the distant provinces without assistance. The French of St Domingo would be more suited for these expeditions than for those which can be made with the assistance of savages, who would not fail to be offended from neglect of the civility which is necessary in order to obtain their goodwill, and from neglect of the reserve which ought to be maintained towards their wives, of whom they are very jealous;—which causes of offence would render useless the greatest chances of success which the French might possess in this enterprise.

It is certain that France would draw from these mines greater benefits than Spain, from the facility of transport, although Spain obtains more than six millions (of *ecus?*) a year. We might also, perhaps, open a passage to the South Sea, which is not more distant than the breadth of the province of

Culiacan, not to mention the possibility of meeting with some rivers near to the Seignelai, which may discharge themselves on that side.

The Sieur de la Salle would not think this affair so easy, if, in addition to his knowledge of their language, he was not familiar with the manners of the savages, through which he may obtain as much confidence by a behaviour in accordance with their practices, as he has impressed on them a feeling of respect in consequence of all that he has yet done in passing with a small number of followers through so many nations, and punishing those who broke their word with him. After this he has no doubt that in a short time they will become good French subjects, so that, without drawing any considerable number of men from Europe, they will form a powerful colony, and will have troops sufficient to act in any emergency, and for the execution of the greatest enterprises. The missionaries of Paraguay and the English of Boston have succeeded so well, that equal success may be expected by the adoption of measures similar to theirs.

Even if the peace of Europe should make it necessary to postpone the execution of this design as respects the conquests proposed, it would always be important to place ourselves in a position to succeed in them when the state of affairs shall change, taking immediate possession of this country in order not to be anticipated by other nations, who will not fail to take advantage of the information which they certainly have, since the Dutch published a statement of the discovery of this country in one of their newspapers more than a year ago.

If, also, the Spaniards should delay satisfying the King at the conclusion of a peace, an expedition at this point will oblige them to hasten its conclusion, and to give to his Majesty important places in Europe in exchange for those which they may lose in a country of the possession of which they are extremely jealous. In order, also, to hasten them, some of their maritime places may be insulted *en passant*, the pillage of which may well repay the expenses of the expedition.

There never was an enterprise of such great importance proposed at so little risk and expense, since the Sieur de la Salle asks only for its execution a vessel of about 30 guns, the power of raising in France 200 men whom he shall think proper for his purpose, and, exclusive of the fitting out of the ship, provisions for six months, some cannon to mount at a fort, the necessary arms and supplies, and wherewith to pay the men for the period of a year. These expenses would be repaid in a short time by the duties which his Majesty might have levied on the articles which would enter into the commerce that would be carried on there, and respecting which a separate memoir has been delivered.

It would not require much time to bring this expedition to an end, since it is nearly certain that the savages can be assembled next winter, and complete this conquest in the spring, in sufficient time to report the news of it by the time the first vessel returns to France.

The Sieur de la Salle does not ask for regular troops. He prefers the assistance of persons of different trades, or at least a majority of such—first, because they will become soldiers when it may be necessary for them to be so; secondly, because, in enterprises of this kind, success depends more on the experience of the commander than on the bravery of those who have only to obey, as was shown in what was done by those who previously accompanied the Sieur de la Salle, the greater part of whom had not seen service; thirdly, this warfare is so different from that carried on in Europe, that the oldest soldiers would be found to be still novices, so that 50 old soldiers to keep the others in order, together with 50 buccaneers, and those whom the Sieur de la Salle has in the country accustomed to such expeditions, will be sufficient to sustain the rest, and to render them capable of any enterprise whatever; fourthly, if only soldiers were taken, it would require double expense to bring to the settlement the necessary labourers; fifthly, the officers who would command the troops, finding a life of greater hardship than they had imagined, and unmixed with any pleasure, would soon be dissatisfied, and this feeling would easily communicate itself to the soldiers when they should discover that there was no relaxation of their fatigues in debauch and licence; sixthly, it would be the ruin of the settlement to commence it with idlers, such as most soldiers are. Far from contributing to the prosperity of a colony, they destroy its most favourable hopes by the disorders which they cause.

It may be objected that the River Seignelai is, perhaps, more distant from New Biscay than has been assumed. To answer this difficulty it is sufficient to mention that the mouth through which it enters the Mississippi is 100 leagues west-north-west from the place where the latter river discharges itself into the Gulf of Mexico, and that it has been ascended more than 60 leagues, going always to the west, after which Monseigneur can judge of the truth of what has been put forth respecting the distance between this river and the province.

The second difficulty which may be raised may be, that peace being concluded, no advantage can be taken of that post. The answer is, that peace is the most proper time to prepare for war when it shall become necessary. Even if peace should prevent us from deriving all the advantages which we may expect from this expense, we should be well remunerated if we choose to profit by the future, because we should have more leisure to conciliate and discipline the savages, and to strengthen the colony, from which circumstance we could obtain more important advantages, and execute more glorious and profitable undertakings (*choses*). It may be feared that we may, at a future time, make an unavailing search for that which we might now abandon to strangers. The injury which the colonies of Hudson Bay and of New England, which were formerly disregarded, do to New France, ought to serve as a warning on this subject.

The third objection respecting the insults which the Spaniards might inflict on the settlement, has already been answered in describing the position which makes it inaccessible by land, and almost equally safe from an attack by water, in consequence of the danger a hostile fleet would incur if it should attempt to advance so far up a very narrow river.

Fourthly, those who do not know the policy of the savages and the knowledge which they have of their true interests, will, perhaps, think it to be dangerous to arm them. But besides the experience which we have of the contrary, not one of the French allies having yet abused the favour (*condescendance*) shown to them for these eighty years, it is certain that those nations which we call savage, know too well the importance to them of having arms for their own defence and for the conquest of their enemies, to make use of them against those who supply them.

Fifthly, it may be said, that should so small a force succeed in driving the Spaniards from this province, it would not be adequate to resist all the forces of Mexico, which they would unite to revenge this affront. The answer to this is, that these forces are not so considerable as is supposed—that they cannot leave unprotected other places—that it will require much time to assemble them ; the diversion which the buccaneers may cause compelling them to provide for the most urgent want,—and that, finally, the Indians, Mulattoes, and Negroes armed and freed by this first success from the terror which they have of the Spaniards, would be able to dispute the advance of the largest army which could be raised in Mexico. Besides which, they would stake all, in order not to be again reduced to a state of slavery.

Sixthly, it is not believed that the expense will be an objection, since it is too inconsiderable in proportion to the great advantages to be hoped for, even if peace should delay their enjoyment. These advantages are of such importance as to make it profitable to incur it for some years rather than to hazard their loss. The enterprise ought not to be delayed to a period when we should no longer have the mastery of it. It is also to be believed that the Spaniards, feeling themselves pushed so closely on that side, would assent to conditions of peace most advantageous to France, and, as has been already stated, the duties which his Majesty could levy on the merchandise, which would be obtained from thence, would repay with usury the expenses incurred.

Seventhly, the Sieur de la Salle would oblige himself, in case the peace should continue for three years and thus prevent him from executing the proposed design, to repay to his Majesty all that may be advanced, or to forfeit the property and government which he shall have created—which he hopes his Majesty will be willing to confirm to him.

NOTE OF WHAT IS REQUISITE FOR THE EXPEDITION.

A vessel of 30 guns, armed and provided with every thing necessary, and the crew paid and supported during the voyage; twelve other pieces of cannon for the two forts of five or six pounds to the ball, and eight cannon of ten or twelve, with the gun carriages and train : two hundred balls for each cannon, and powder in proportion.

A hundred picked men, levied at the expense of his Majesty, but selected by the Sieur de la Salle. Their pay for one year to be 120 (?) a man, and as the money would be of no avail to them in the colony, it shall be converted at the place of embarcation into goods (*denrées*) proper for them.

The pay, during six months, of 100 (?) for the other men, enlisted by the Sieur de la Salle, to be paid by his Majesty during the time they shall be employed in the proposed conquest.

Victuals for all during six months ; 600 musquets for arming 400 savages, in addition to 1,600 who are already armed, and the others for the 200 Frenchmen.

A hundred pair of pistols proper to be worn in the girdle ; 150 swords and as many sabres, 25 pikes (*pertuisanes*), 25 halberds, 20,000 lbs. of gunpowder, four to five (?) of which to be given to each savage, and the remainder left in the forts, and for the use of the French during the expedition.

Musquet balls of the proper calibre in proportion; gun-worms, powder-horns, rifle-flints, 300 to 400 grenades, six petards of the smallest and lightest kind, pincers, pickaxes, hoes, hones, shovels, axes, hatchets, and cramp-irons for the fortifications and buildings; 5,000 to 6,000 lbs. of iron and 400 lbs. of steel of all sorts. A forge with its appurtenances, besides the tools necessary for armourers, joiners, coopers, wheel-wrights, carpenters, and masons.

Two boxes of surgery provided with medicine and instruments.

Two chapels and the ornaments for the almoners.

A barge of 40 tons in pieces (*en fagots*), or built with its appurtenances.

Refreshments for the sick.

LETTERS PATENT

TRANSLATION.

Louis, by the grace of God, King of France and of Navarre. To our dear and well-beloved Robert Cavelier, Sieur de la Salle, greeting.

We have received with favor the very humble petition, which has been presented to us in your name, to permit you to endeavour to discover the western part of New France; and we have consented to this proposal the more willingly, because there is nothing we have more at heart than the discovery of this country, through which it is probable a road may be found to penetrate to Mexico (*dans laquel il y a apparence que l'on trouvera un chemin pour penetrer jusqu'au Mexique;*) and because your diligence in clearing the lands which we granted to you by the decree of our council of the 13th of May, 1675, and, by Letters Patent of the same date, to form habitations upon the said lands, and to put Fort Frontenac in a good state of defence, the seigniory and government whereof we likewise granted to you, affords us every reason to hope that you will succeed to our satisfaction, and to the advantage of our subjects of the said country.

For these reasons, and others thereunto moving us, we have permitted, and do hereby permit you, by these presents, signed by our hand, to endeavour to discover the western part of New France, and, for the execution of this enterprise, to construct forts where-ever you shall deem it necessary; which it is our will that you shall hold on the same terms and conditions as Fort Frontenac, agreeably and conformably to our said Letters Patent of the 13th of March, 1675, which we have confirmed, as far as is needful, and hereby confirm by these presents. And it is our pleasure that they be executed according to their form and tenor.

To accomplish this, and everything above mentioned, we give you full powers; on condition, however, that you shall finish this enterprise within five years, in default of which these presents shall be void and of none effect; that you carry on no trade whatever with the savages called Outaouacs, and others who bring their beaver skins and other peltries to Montreal; and that the whole shall be done at your expense, and that of your company, to which we have granted the privilege of the trade in buffalo skins. And we command the Sieur de Frontenac, our Governor and Lieutenant-General, and the Sieur Duchesne Intendant, and the other officers who compose the supreme council of the said country, to affix their signatures to these presents; for such is our pleasure. Given at St Germain en Laye, this 12th day of May, 1678, and of our reign the thirty-fifth.

(Signed)   LOUIS.

And lower down,

By the King,

COLBERT.

And sealed with the great seal with yellow wax.

The act of the Governor, attached to these presents, is dated the 5th of November, 1678.*

---

* I have a M.S. copy of the original in French, and have corrected the translation which was published by Mr Sparks in 1844.

" MEMOIR OF THE SIEUR DE LA SALLE REPORT-
ING TO MONSIEGNEUR DE SEIGNELAY THE
DISCOVERIES MADE BY HIM UNDER THE ORDER
OF HIS MAJESTY.

MONSEIGNEUR COLBERT was of opinion, with regard to the various propositions which were made in
1678, that it was important for the glory and service
of the King to discover a port for his vessels in the
Gulf of Mexico.

The Sieur de la Salle offered to undertake the discovery, at his own expense, if it should please his
Majesty to grant to him the Seignory of the government of the forts which he should erect on his route,
together with certain privileges as an indemnification
for the great outlay which the expedition would im-
pose on him. Such grant was made to him by letters
patent of the 12th of May, 1678.

In order to execute this commission, he abandoned
all his own pursuits which did not relate to it. He
did not omit anything necessary for success, notwithstanding dangerous sickness, considerable losses, and
other misfortunes which he suffered, which would
have discouraged any other person not possessed of
the same zeal with himself, and the same industry in
the performance of the undertaking. He has made

five voyages under extraordinary hardships, extending over more than 5,000 leagues, most commonly on foot, through snow and water, almost without rest, during five years. He has traversed more than 600 leagues of unknown country, among many barbarous and cannibal nations (antropophages), against whom he was obliged to fight almost daily, although he was accompanied by only 36 men, having no other consolation before him than a hope of bringing to an end an enterprise which he believed would be agreeable to his Majesty.

After having happily executed this design, he hopes Monseigneur will be pleased to continue him in the title (*propriété*) and government of the fort which he has had erected in the country of his discovery, where he has placed several French settlers—and has brought together many savage nations, amounting to more than 18,000 in number, who have built houses there and sown much ground—to commence a powerful colony.

This is the only fruit of an expenditure of 150,000 *eçus*—the only means of satisfying his creditors who advanced to him the aid which he required after very considerable losses.

He believes that he has sufficiently established the truth of his discovery by the official instrument signed*

---

* See this *Proces verbal*, of the existence of which I was not aware when I printed this passage in the Journal of the Royal Geographical Society. The document was first printed by Mr Jared Sparks, of Boston, and I have reprinted it with these Memoirs.

by all his companions, which was placed last year in the hands of Monseigneur Colbert by the Count de Frontenac:—as also by a report drawn up by the Reverend Father Zenoble, Missionary, who accompanied him during this voyage, and who is at this time Guardian of Bapaume:—by the testimony of three persons who accompanied him, and whom he has brought with him to France, and who are now in Paris:—and by the testimony of many other persons who came this year from Canada, and who have seen one Vital, sent by M. de la Barre to collect information respecting him, on the spot, and who has confirmed the truth of the discovery.

All these proofs are sufficient to contradict whatever may have been written to the contrary, by persons who have no knowledge of the country where the discovery was made—never having been there. But he hopes to remove all these prejudices, by carrying into execution the design which he entertains, under the favour of Monseigneur, of returning to the country of his discovery by the mouth of the river in the Gulf of Mexico, since he must have lost his sense, if, without being certain of the means of arriving where he proposes, he exposed not only his own fortune and that of his friends to manifest destruction, but his own honour and reputation to the unavoidable disgrace of having imposed on the confidence of his Majesty and of his ministers. Of this there is less likelihood, because he has no interest to disguise the

truth, since, if Monseigneur does not think it convenient to undertake any enterprise in that direction
he will not ask anything more from his Majesty,
until his return from the Gulf of Mexico confirms
the truth of what he has alleged. With reference
to the assertion, that his voyage would produce no
profit to France, he replies, that if he proposed it
as a thing to be done, and on that account sought for
assistance to undertake the enterprise, or reward after
having succeeded in it, its usefulness would deserve
consideration; but being here only in order to render
an account of the orders he received, he does not think
himself to be responsible for anything but their execution, it not being his duty to examine the intentions of
Monseigneur Colbert. Having, however, observed
great advantages which both France and Canada may
derive from his discovery, he believes that he owes
this detail to the glory of the King, the welfare of the
kingdom—to the honour of the Ministry of Monsiegneur, and to the memory of him who employed
him upon this expedition. He does this the more
willingly, as his requests will not expose him to a
suspicion of self-interest; and as the influence which
he has acquired over the people of that continent places
him in a position to execute what he proposes, the
things which he states will find greater credit in the
minds of those who shall investigate them.

Firstly, the service of God may be established there
by the preaching of the Gospel to numerous docile

and settled (*sedentaires*) nations, who will be found more willing to receive it than those of other parts of America, upon account of their greater civilization. They have already temples and a form of worship.

Secondly, we can effect there for the glory of our King very important conquests, both by land and by sea; or if peace should oblige us to delay the execution of them, we might, without giving any cause of complaint, make preparations to render us certain of success whenever it shall please the King to command it.

The provinces which may be seized are very rich in silver mines—they adjoin the River Colbert (the Mississippi)—they are far removed from succour—they are open everywhere on the side on which we should attack them and are defended only by a small number of persons, so sunk in effeminancy and indolence as to be incapable of enduring the fatigue of wars of this description.

The Sieur de la Salle binds himself to have this enterprise ripe for success within one year after his arrival on the spot, and asks only for this purpose one vessel, some arms, and munitions, the transport, maintenance, and pay of 200 men during one year. Afterwards he will maintain them from the produce of the country and supply their other wants through the credit and confidence which he has obtained among those nations, and the experience which he has had of those regions. He will give a more detailed account of this proposal when it shall please Monseigneur to direct him.

Thirdly, the river is navigable for more than a hundred leagues for ships, and for barks for more than 500 leagues to the north, and for more than 800 from east to west. Its three mouths are as many harbours, capable of receiving every description of ships; where those of his Majesty will always find a secure retreat, and all that may be necessary to refit, and re-victual—which would be a great economy to his Majesty, who would no longer find it necessary to send the things needed from France at a great expense, the country producing the greater part of them. We could even build there as many ships as we should desire, the materials for building and rigging them being in abundance, with the exception of iron, which may perhaps be discovered.

In the first place we should obtain there everything which has enriched New England and Virginia, and which constitute the foundation of their commerce and of their great wealth—timber of every kind—salted meat, tallow, corn, sugar, tobacco, honey, wax, resin, and other gums; immense pasturages, hemp, and other articles with which more than 200 vessels are every year freighted in New England to carry elsewhere.

The newly-discovered country has, besides its other advantages, that of the soil, which, being only partly

covered with wood, forms a campaign of great fer-
tility and extent, scarcely requiring any clearing.
The mildness of the climate is favourable to the rearing of a large number of cattle, which cause great
expense where the winter is severe. There is also a
prodigious number (*plus un nombre prodigieux*) of
buffaloes, stags, hinds, roes, bears, otters, lynxes.
Hides and furs are to be had there almost for
nothing (*à vil prix*), the savages not yet knowing the
value of our commodities. There are cotton, cochineal,
nuts, turnsols—entire forests of mulberry-trees—salt,
slate, coal, vines, apple-trees; so that it would be easy
to make wine, cyder, oil of nuts, of turnsols, and of
olives also, if olive-trees were planted there, silk, and
dye-woods. It will not be necessary to import from
Europe horses, oxen, swine, fowls, or turkies, which
are to be found in different parts of the country, nor
to import provisions for the colonists, who would
quickly find subsistence.

Whilst other colonies are open and exposed to the
descents of foreigners by as many points as their coasts
are washed by the sea, whereby they are placed under
a necessity of having many persons to watch these
points of access; one single post, established towards
the lower part of the river, will be sufficient to protect
a territory extending more than 800 leagues from
north to south, and still farther from east to west,
because its banks are only accessible from the sea
through the mouth of the river, the remainder of the

coast being impenetrable inland for more than 20 leagues, in consequence of woods, bogs, reeds, and marshes (*terres tremblantes*), through which it is impossible to march; and this may be the reason why the exploration of that river has been neglected by the Spaniards, if they have had any knowledge of it. This country is equally well defended in the interior against the irruptions of neighbouring Europeans, by great chains of mountains stretching from east to west, from which branches of the river take their source.

It is true that the country is more open towards the south-west, where it borders on Mexico, where the very navigable river the Seignelay, which is one of the branches of the Colbert (the Mississippi) is only separated by a forest of three to four days' journey in depth. But besides that the Spaniards there are feeble and far removed from the assistance of Mexico, and from that which they could expect by sea, this place is protected from their insults by a great number of warlike savages, who close this passage to them, and who, constantly engaged with them in cruel wars, would certainly inflict greater evil when sustained by some French, whose more mild and more humane mode of governing will prove a great means for the preservation of the peace made between them and the Sieur de la Salle.

To maintain this establishment, which is the only one required in order to obtain all the advantages mentioned, 200 men only are needed, who would also construct the fortifications and buildings, and effect the clearings necessary for the sustenance of the colony ; after which there would be no further expenditure. The goodness of the country will induce the settlers (*habitans*) to remain there willingly. The ease in which they will live will make them attend to the cultivation of the soil, and to the production of articles of commerce, and will remove all desire to imitate the inhabitants of New France, who are obliged to seek subsistence in the woods under great fatigues, in hunting for peltries which are their principal resource. These vagrant courses, common in New France, will be easily prevented in the new country, because, as its rivers are all navigable, there will be a great facility for the savages to come to our settlements and for us to go to them in boats which can ascend all the branches of the river.

If foreigners anticipate us, they will deprive France of all the advantages to be expected from the success of the enterprise. They will complete the ruin of New France, which they already hem in through Virginia, Pennsylvania, New England, and the Hudson's Bay. They will not fail to ascend the river as high as possible, and to establish colonies in the places nearest to the savages who now bring their furs to Montreal—they will make constant inroads into the countries of the latter, which could not be repressed by ordinances of his Majesty. They have already made several attempts to discover this passage, and they will not neglect it now that the whole world knows that it is discovered, since the Dutch have published it in their newspapers upwards of a year ago. Nothing more is required than to maintain the possession taken by the Sieur de la Salle, in order to deprive them of such a desire, and to place ourselves in a position to undertake enterprises against them glorious to the arms of his Majesty, who will probably derive the greatest benefits from the duties he will levy there, as in our other colonies.

Even if this affair should prove hurtful to New France, it will contribute to its security, and render our commerce in furs more considerable.

There will be nothing to fear from the Iroquois when the nations of the south, strengthened through their intercourse with the French, shall stop their conquests, and prevent their being powerful, by carrying off a great number of their women and children, which they can easily do from the inferiority of the weapons of their enemies. As respects commerce, that post will probably increase our traffic still more than has been done by the establishment of Fort Frontenac, which was built with success for that purpose, for if the Illinois and their allies were to catch the beavers, which the Iroquois now kill in their neighbourhood in order to carry to the English, the latter, not being any longer able to get them from their own colonies, would be obliged to buy them from us, to the great benefit of those who have the privilege of this traffic.

These were the views which the Sieur de la Salle had in placing the settlement where it is. The colony has already felt its effects, as all our allies, who had fled after the departure of M. de Frontenac, have returned to their ancient dwellings, in consequence of the confidence caused by the fort, near which they have defeated a party of Iroquois, and have built four other forts to protect themselves from hostile incursions. The Governor, M. de la Barre, and the Intendant, M. de Meulles, have told the Sieur de la Salle that they would write to Monseigneur to inform him of the importance of that fort in order to keep the Iroquois in check, and that M. de Lagny had proposed its establishment in 1678. Monseigneur Colbert permitted Sieur de la Salle to build it, and granted it to him as a property.* In order to prove to Monseigneur the sincerity of his intentions still more, and that he had no other motive in selecting this site than the protection of the men he has left there, and whom he did not think right to place in such small number, within the reach of the Spaniards, and without cannon and munition, or to leave in so distant a country, where in case of sickness they could expect no assistance, nor to return home from thence without danger—he offers again to descend the river a hundred leagues lower

---

* The fort of St Louis on the Illinois?

down, and nearer the sea, and to establish there another fort, demolishing the first, in the expectation, however, that Monseigneur would consider the expenses incurred in its establishment.

It may be said, firstly, that this colony might injure the commerce of Quebec, and cause the desertion of its inhabitants ; but the answer is, that by descending lower down, no beavers will be found. Thus the first difficulty will be removed, which again would not have any foundation, even if Fort St Louis were to remain. The Illinois will only kill the beaver, which, after their departure, would fall to the share of the Iroquois only, as no other nation dares to approach those districts. There is also no likelihood that deserters would choose a long and difficult route, at the end of which they would be still subject to be apprehended and punished, whilst they have another much shorter and easier one to New England, where they are quite secure, and which many take every year.

A second objection would be, that the goodness of the country would attract so many people as to diminish the population of France, as it is said Mexico and Peru have depopulated Spain ; but, besides that France is more peopled than Spain has ever been, and that the expulsion of 1,800,000 Moors, added to the great wars she has had to sustain, is the real cause of its diminished population. It is certain that the number of the few Spaniards in those kingdoms, who are not above 40,000, is not a number of emigrants sufficient to make any perceptible change in France, which already counts more than 100,000 settlers in foreign countries. It would be even desirable that instead of peopling other foreign kingdoms, the riches of the country newly discovered should attract them to it. Moreover, this objection has already been answered, when it was said that the country can be defended by one or two forts, for the protection of which only from 400 to 500 men are required, a number comprising only one half of the crew of a large vessel.

Whatever has been imagined respecting the mud and breakers which are supposed to stop the mouth of the river, is easily disproved by the experience of those who have been there, and who found the entrances fine, deep, and capable of admitting the largest vessels. It would appear that the land or *levées de terre* are covered in many parts with wood growing along the channel of the river very far into the sea; and where the sea is deep they would not be suspected, because even the creeks of the sea are tolerably deep at that distance, and besides, there is every appearance that the current of the river has formed these kind of dikes, by shoving on both sides the mud with which the winds fill the neighbouring creeks, because those causeways are to the right and left of the river, forming for it a bed, as it were, by their separation. Nor can it be believed that these *levées** will ever change their position, since they consist of a hard soil, covered with pretty large trees following regularly the banks of the river, which form the bed of it for more than six leagues into the sea.

In the memoir respecting New Biscay, the difficulty has been dealt with respecting the inconstancy of the savages. They know too well how important it is to them to live on good terms with us, to fail in their fidelity, in which they have never been known to fail in New France. Such an event is still less to be apprehended from those who are obedient and submissive to their *caziques,* whose good-will it is sufficient to gain, in order to keep the rest in obedience.

---

* This word is in local use at New Orleans, to describe both the great artificial embankment of the river and any natural embankment.

"PROCES VERBAL.

"Of the taking Possession of Louisiana, at the Mouth of the Mississippi, by the Sieur de la Salle, on the 9th of April, 1682.*

"Jaques de la Metairie, Notary of Fort Frontenac in New France, commissioned to exercise the said function of Notary during the voyage to Louisiana, in North America, by M. de la Salle, Governor of Fort Frontenac for the King, and commandant of the said Discovery by the commission of his Majesty given at St Germain, on the 12th of May, 1678.

"To all those to whom these presents shall come, greeting;—Know, that having been requested by the said Sieur de la Salle to deliver to him an act, signed by us and by the witnesses therein named, of possession by him taken of the country of Louisiana, near the three mouths of the Rivert Colbert, in the Gulf of Mexico, on the 9th of April, 1682.

"In the name of the most high, mighty, invincible,

---

* "This curious and important historical document has never been printed. The translation here given is made from the original, contained in the archives of the Marine Department at Paris. The proper names remain precisely as they are found in the manuscript, although the orthography of several of them is different from that which was afterwards adopted."—*Note by Mr Sparks on its publication at Boston in* 1844.

and victorious Prince, Louis the Great, by the Grace of God, King of France and of Navarre, Fourteenth of that name, and of his heirs, and the successor of his crown, we, the aforesaid Notary, have delivered the said act to the said Sieur de la Salle, the tenor whereof follows.

" On the 27th of December, 1681, M. de la Salle departed on foot to join M. de Tonty, who had preceded him with his followers and all his equipage 40 leagues into the Miamis country, where the ice on the River Chekagou, in the country of the Mascoutens, had arrested his progress, and where, when the ice became stronger, they used sledges to drag the baggage, the canoes, and a wounded Frenchman, through the whole length of this river, and on the Illinois, a distance of 70 leagues.

" At length, all the French being together, on the 25th of January, 1682, we came to Pimiteoui. From that place, the river being frozen only in some parts, we continued our route to the River Colbert, 60 leagues, or thereabouts, from Pimiteoui, and 90 leagues, or thereabouts, from the village of the Illinois. We reached the banks of the River Colbert on the 6th of January, and remained there until the 13th, waiting for the savages, whose progress had been impeded by the ice. On the 13th, all having assembled, we renewed our voyage, being 22 French, carrying arms, accompanied by the Reverend Father Zenobe Membré, one of the Recollet Missionaries,

and followed by 18 New England savages, and several women, Ilgonquines, Otchipoises, and Huronnes.

" On the 14th, we arrived at the village of Maroa,
consisting of a hundred cabins, without inhabitants.
Proceeding about a hundred leagues down the River
Colbert, we went ashore to hunt on the 26th of February. A Frenchman was lost in the woods, and it
was reported to M. de la Salle, that a large number
of savages had been seen in the vicinity. Thinking
that they might have seized the Frenchman, and in
order to observe these savages, he marched through
the woods during two days, but without finding them,
because they had all been frightened by the guns
which they had heard, and had fled.

" Returning to camp, he sent in every direction
French and savages on the search, with orders, if they
fell in with savages, to take them alive without injury,
that he might gain from them intelligence of this
Frenchman. Gabriel Barbié, with two savages, having
met five of the Chikacha nation, captured two of them.
They were received with all possible kindness, and,
after he had explained to them that he was anxious
about a Frenchman who had been lost, and that he
only detained them that he might rescue him from
their hands, if he was really among them, and afterwards make with them an advantageous peace (the
French doing good to everybody), they assured him
that they had not seen the man whom we sought, but
that peace would be received with the greatest satis-

faction. Presents were then given to them, and, as they had signified that one of their villages was not more than half a day's journey distant, M. de la Salle set out the next day to go thither; but, after travelling till night, and having remarked that they often contradicted themselves in their discourse, he declined going farther, without more provisions. Having pressed them to tell the truth, they confessed that it was yet four days' journey to their villages; and, perceiving that M. de la Salle was angry at having been deceived, they proposed that one of them should remain with him, while the other carried the news to the village, whence the elders would come and join them four days' journey below that place. The said Sieur de la Salle returned to the camp with one of these Chikachas; and the Frenchman, whom we sought, having been found, he continued his voyage, and passed the river of the Chepontias, and the village of the Metsigameas. The fog, which was very thick, prevented his finding the passage which led to the rendezvous proposed by the Chikachas.

" On the 12th of March, we arrived at the Kapaha village of Akansa. Having established a peace there, and taken possession, we passed, on the 15th, another of their villages, situate on the border of their river, and also two others, farther off in the depth of the forest, and arrived at that of Imaha, the largest village in this nation, where peace was confirmed, and where the chief acknowledged that the village belonged to his Majesty. Two Akansas embarked with M. de la Salle to conduct him to the Talusas, their allies, about 50 leagues distant, who inhabit eight villages upon the borders of a little lake. On the 19th, we passed the villages of Tourika, Jason, and Kouera; but, as they did not border on the river, and were hostile to the Akansas and Taensas, we did not stop there.

" On the 20th, we arrived at the Taensas, by whom we were exceedingly well received, and supplied with a large quantity of provisions. M. de Tonty passed a night at one of their villages, where there were about 700 men carrying arms, assembled in the place. Here again a peace was concluded. A peace was also made with the Koroas, whose chief came there from the principal village of the Koroas, two leagues distant from that of the Natches. The two chiefs accompanied M. de la Salle to the banks of the river. Here the Koroa chief embarked with him, to conduct him to his village, where peace was again concluded with this nation, which, besides the five other villages of which it is composed, is allied to nearly 40 others. On the 31st, we passed the village of the Oumas without knowing it, on account of the fog, and its distance from the river.

" On the 3rd of April, at about 10 o'clock in the morning, we saw among the canes 13 or 14 canoes. M. de la Salle landed, with several of his people. Footprints were seen, and also savages, a little lower down, who were fishing, and who fled precipitately as soon as they discovered us. Others of our party then went ashore on the borders of a marsh formed by the inundation of the river. M. de la Salle sent two Frenchmen, and then two savages, to reconnoitre, who reported that there was a village not far off, but that the whole of this marsh, covered with canes, must be crossed to reach it; that they had been assailed with a shower of arrows by the inhabitants of the town, who had not dared to engage with them in the marsh, but who had then withdrawn, although neither the French nor the savages with them had fired, on account of the orders they had received not to act unless in pressing danger. Presently we heard a drum beat in the village, and the cries and howlings with which these barbarians are accustomed to make attacks. We waited three or four hours, and, as we could not encamp in this marsh, and seeing no one, and no longer hearing anything, we embarked.

" An hour afterwards, we came to the village of Maheouala, lately destroyed, and containing dead bodies and marks of blood. Two leagues below this place we encamped. We continued our voyage till the 6th, when we discovered three channels by which the River Colbert discharges itself into the sea. We landed on the bank of the most western channel, about three leagues from its mouth. On the 7th, M. de la Salle went to reconnoitre the shores of the neighbouring sea, and M. de Tonty likewise examined the great middle channel. They found these two outlets beautiful, large, and deep. On the 8th, we reascended the river, a little above its confluence with the sea, to find a dry place, beyond the reach of inundations. The elevation of the North Pole was here about 27°. Here we prepared a column and a cross, and to the said column were affixed the arms of France, with this inscription:

LOUIS LE GRAND, ROI DE FRANCE ET DE NA-
VARRE, RÈGNE; LE NEUVIÈME AVRIL, 1682.

The whole party, under arms, chanted the *Te Deum*, the *Exaudiat*, the *Domine salvum fac Regem*; and then, after a salute of fire arms and cries of *Vive le Roi*, the column was erected by M. de la Salle, who, standing near it, said, with a loud voice, in French:—
' In the name of the most high, mighty, invincible, and victorious Prince, Louis the Great, by the Grace of God King of France and of Navarre, Fourteenth of that name, this ninth day of April, one thousand six hundred and eighty-two, I, in virtue of the commission of his Majesty which I hold in my hand, and which may be seen by all whom it may concern, have taken, and do now take, in the name of his Majesty and of his successors to the crown, possession of this country of Louisiana, the seas, harbours, ports, bays, adjacent straits; and all the nations, people, provinces, cities, towns, villages, mines, minerals, fisheries, streams, and rivers, comprised in the extent of the said Louisiana, from the mouth of the great river St Louis, on the

eastern side, otherwise called Ohio, Alighin, Sipore, or Chukagona, and this with the consent of the Chaouanons, Chikachas, and other people dwelling therein, with whom we have made alliance; as also along the River Colbert, or Mississippi, and rivers which discharge themselves therein, from its source beyond the country of the Kious or Nadouessious, and this with their consent, and with the consent of the Motantees, Ilinois, Mesigameas, Natches, Koroas, which are the most considerable nations dwelling therein, with whom also we have made alliance, either by ourselves or by others in our behalf;* as far as its mouth at the sea, or Gulf of Mexico, about the 27th degree of the elevation of the North Pole, and also to the mouth of River of Palms; upon the assurance which we have received from all these nations, that we are the first Europeans who have descended or ascended the said River Colbert; hereby protesting against all those who may in future undertake to invade any or all of these countries, people, or lands, above described, to the prejudice of the right of his Majesty, acquired by the consent of the nations herein named. Of which, and of all that can be needed, I

---

* " There is an obscurity in this enumeration of places and Indian nations, which may be ascribed to an ignorance of the geography of the country ; but it seems to be the design of the Sieur de la Salle to take possession of the whole territory watered by the Mississippi from its mouth to its source, and by the streams flowing into it on both sides."—*Note by Mr Sparks.*

hereby take to witness those who hear me, and demand an act of the Notary, as required by law.'

"To which the whole assembly responded with shouts of *Vive le Roi,* and with salutes of fire arms. Moreover, the said Sieur de la Salle caused to be buried at the foot of the tree, to which the cross was attached, a leaden plate, on one side of which were engraved the arms of France, and the following Latin inscription :—

LVDOVICVS MAGNVS REGNAT.

NONO APRILIS CIƆ IƆC LXXXII.

ROBERTVS CAVELIER, CVM DOMINO DE TONTY, LEGATO, R. P. ZENOBIO MEMBRÈ, RECOLLECTO, ET VIGINTI GALLIS, PRIMVS HOC FLVMEN, INDE AB ILINEORVM PAGO, ENAVIGAVIT, EJVSQVE OSTIVM FECIT PERVIVM, NONO APRILIS ANNI CIƆ IƆC LXXXII.

After which the Sieur de la Salle said, that his Majesty, as eldest son of the Church, would annex no country to his crown, without making it his chief care to establish the Christian religion therein, and that its symbol must now be planted; which was accordingly done at once by erecting a cross, before which the *Vexilla* and the *Domine salvum fac Regem* were sung. Whereupon the ceremony was concluded with cries of *Vive le Roi.*

"Of all and every of the above, the said Sieur de la Salle having required of us an instrument, we have delivered to him the same, signed by us, and by the undersigned witnesses, this ninth day of April, one thousand six hundred and eighty-two.

" LA METAIRIE,

" *Notary*.

" DE LA SALLE.

" P. ZENOBE, *Recollet Missionary*.

" HENRY DE TONTY.

" FRANÇOIS DE BOISRONDET.

" JEAN BOURDON.

" SIEUR D'AUTRAY.

" JAQUES CAUCHOIS.

" PIERRE YOU.

" GILLES MEUCRET.

" JEAN MICHEL, *Surgeon*.

" JEAN MAS.

" JEAN DULIGNON.

" NICOLAS DE LA SALLE."

⁎ The above is reprinted from Mr Sparks's ' Life of La Salle,' published at Boston, Massachusetts, in 1844. The original document, in French, has not been published.

WILL OF THE SIEUR DE LA SALLE.

ROBERT CAVELIER,* Esquire, Sieur de la Salle, Seigneur and Governor of the Fort Frontenac in New France, considering the great dangers and continual perils in which the voyages I undertake engage me, and wishing to acknowledge, as much as I am able, the great obligations which I owe to M. François Plet, my cousin for the signal services which he has rendered to me in my most pressing necessities, and because it is through his assistance that I have preserved to this time Fort Frontenac against the efforts which were made to deprive me of it, I have given, granted, and transferred, and give, grant, and transfer, by these presents, to the said M. Plet, in case of my death, the seigniory and property of the ground and limits of the said Fort Frontenac and its depending lands, and all my rights in the country of the Miamis, Illinois, and others to the south, together with the establishment which is in the country of the Miamis,

---

* The value of this document before the publication of the *Proces Verbal* by Mr Sparks, was, that in connexion with the letters of La Salle, written in 1683, it determined the year in which the discovery of the mouth of the Mississippi was made. I used it for this purpose in an article written for the Journal of the Royal Geographical Society, before Mr Sparks's work was published.

in the condition which it shall be at the time of my death, that of Niagara, and all the others which I may have founded there, together with all barges, boats, great boats, moveables, and immoveables, rights, privileges, rents, lands, buildings, and other things belonging to me which shall be found there; willing that these presents be, and serve for my testament and declaration in the manner in which I ought to make it, such being my last will as above written by my hand, and signed by my hand, after having read it and again read it (*lu et relu*).

Made at Montreal, the 11th of August, 1681.

(Signed)   CAVELIER DE LA SALLE.

" MEMOIR SENT IN 1693, ON THE DISCOVERY
OF THE MISSISSIPPI AND THE NEIGH-
BOURING NATIONS BY M. DE LA SALLE,
FROM THE YEAR 1678 TO THE TIME OF
HIS DEATH, AND BY THE SIEUR DE TONTY
TO THE YEAR 1691."

MEMOIR, ETC.

After having been eight years in the French service, by land and by sea, and having had a hand shot off in Sicily by a grenade, I resolved to return to France to solicit employment. At that time the late M. Cavelier de la Salle came to Court, a man of great intelligence and merit who sought to obtain leave to discover the Gulf of Mexico by crossing the southern countries of North America. Having obtained of the King the permission he desired through the favour of the late M. Colbert and M. de Seignelai, the late Monseigneur the Prince Conty, who was acquainted with him and who honoured me with his favour, directed me to him to be allowed to accompany him in his long journeys, which he very willingly assented to. We sailed from Rochelle on the 14th of July, 1678, and arrived at Quebec on the 15th of September following. We recruited there for some days, and after having taken leave of M. de Frontenac, ascended the St Lawrence as far as Fort Frontenac (Kingston), 120 leagues from Quebec on the banks of the Lake Frontenac (Lake Ontario,) which is

c

about 300 leagues round. After staying there four
days, we embarked in a boat of 40 tons burthen to
cross the lake, and on Christmas day we were opposite
a village called Isonnoutouan to which M. de la
Salle sent some canoes to procure Indian corn for our
subsistence. From thence we sailed towards Niagara,
intending to look for a place above the Falls where a
boat might be built. The winds were so contrary
that we could not approach it nearer than nine
leagues, which obliged us to go by land. We found
there some cabins of the Iroquois, who received us
well. We slept there, and the next day we went three
leagues further up to look for a good place to build a
boat, and there encamped. The boat we came in
was lost through the obstinacy of the pilot, whom
M. de la Salle had ordered to bring it ashore. The
crew and the things in it were saved. M. de la Salle
determined to return to Fort Frontenac over the ice,
and I remained in command at Niagara with a
Father Recollet and 30 men. The boat was completed in the spring. M. de la Salle joined us
with two other boats and several men to assist us to
work the boat up the Rapids, which I was not able to
ascend on account of the weakness of my crew. He
directed me to proceed and wait for him at the ex-
tremity of Lake Erie, at a place called Detroit, 120
leagues from Niagara, to join some Frenchmen
whom he had sent off the last autumn. I embarked in a canoe of bark, and when we were near

Detroit the boat came up. We got into it, and continued our voyage as far as Michilimakinac, where we arrived at the end of August, having crossed two lakes larger than that of Frontenac (Ontario). We remained there some days to rest ourselves, and as M. de la Salle intended to go to the Illinois, he sent me to the Falls of St Mary, which is situated where Lake Superior discharges itself into Lake Huron, to look for some men who had deserted, and he in the meantime sailed for the Lake Illinois. Having arrived at Poutouatamis, an Illinois village, the calumet was sung, during which ceremony presents are given and received. There is a post placed in the midst of the assembly, where those who wish to make known their great deeds in war, striking the post, declaim on the deeds they have done. This ceremony takes place in presence of those with whom they wish to make friendship, the calumet being the symbol of peace. M. de la Salle sent his boat back to Niagara to fetch the things he wanted, and, embarking in a canoe, continued his voyage to the Miamis River, and there commenced building a house. In the meantime I came up with the deserters, and brought them back to within 30 leagues of the Miamis River, where I was obliged to leave my men, in order to hunt, our provisions failing us. I then went on to join M. de la Salle. When I arrived he told me he wished that all the men had come with me in order that he might proceed to the

Illinois. I therefore retraced my way to find them, but the violence of the wind forced me to land and our canoe was upset by the violence of the waves. It was, however, saved, but everything that was in it was lost, and for want of provisions we lived for three days on acorns. I sent word of what had happened to M. de la Salle and he directed me to join him. I went back in my little canoe and as soon as I arrived we ascended 25 leagues, as far as the portage, where the men whom I had left behind joined us. We made the portage which extends about two leagues and came to the source of the Illinois River. We embarked there and descending the river for 100 leagues arrived at a village of the savages. They were absent hunting and as we had no provisions we opened some *caches** of Indian corn.

During this journey some of our Frenchmen were so fatigued that they determined to leave us, but the night they intended to go was so cold that their plan was broken up. We continued our route, in order to join the savages and found them 30 leagues

---

* " The term *cache*, meaning a place of concealment, was originally used by the French Canadian trappers and traders. It is made by digging a hole in the ground, somewhat in the shape of a jug, which is lined with dry sticks, grass, or anything else that will protect its contents from the dampness of the earth. In this place the goods to be concealed are carefully stowed away."—*Gregg's Commerce of the Prairies*, vol. i, p. 68.

above the village. When they saw us they thought we were Iroquois, and put themselves on the defensive and made their women run into the woods; but when they recognised us the women were called back with their children and the calumet was danced to M. de la Salle and me, in order to mark their desire to live in peace with us. We gave them some merchandise for the corn which he had taken in their village. This was on the 3rd of January, 1679.

As it was necessary to fortify ourselves during the winter we made a fort which was called *Crevecœur.* Part of our people deserted and they had even put poison into our kettle. M. de la Salle was poisoned but he was saved by some antidote a friend had given to him in France. The desertion of these men gave us less annoyance than the effect which it had on the minds of the savages. The enemies of M. de la Salle had spread a report among the Illinois that we were friends of the Iroquois, who are their greatest enemies. The effect this produced will be seen hereafter.

M. de la Salle commenced building a boat to descend the river. He sent a Father Recollet, with the Sieur Deau, to discover the nation of the Sioux, 400 leagues from the Illinois on the Mississippi River southwards, a river that runs not less than 800 leagues to the sea without rapids. He determined to go himself by land to Fort Frontenac because he had heard nothing of the boat which he had sent to Niagara. He gave me the command of this place and left us on the 22nd of March with five men. On his road he met with two men, whom he had sent in the autumn to Michilimakinac to obtain news of his boat. They assured him that it had not come down and he therefore determined to continue his journey. The two men were sent to me with orders to go to the old village to visit a high rock and to build a strong fort upon it. Whilst I was proceeding thither all my men deserted and took away everything that was most valuable. They left me with two Recollets and three men, newly arrived from France, stripped of everything and at the mercy of the savages. All that I could do was to send an authentic account of the affair to M. de la Salle. He laid wait for them on Lake Frontenac, took some of them and killed others, after which he returned to the Illinois. As for his boat, it was never heard of.

During the time this happened the Illinois were greatly alarmed at seeing a party of 600 Iroquois. It was then near the month of September. The desertion of our men, and the journey of M. de la Salle to Fort Frontenac, made the savages suspect that we intended to betray them. They severely reproached me on the arrival of their enemies. As I was so recently come from France and was not then acquainted with their manners, I was embarrassed at this event and determined to go to the enemy with necklaces, and to tell them that I was surprised they should come to make war with a nation dependent on the government of New France, and which M. de la Salle, whom they esteemed, governed. An Illinois accompanied me, and we separated ourselves from the body of the Illinois, who, to the number of 400 only, were fighting with the enemy. When I was within gun-shot the Iroquois shot at us, seized me, took the necklace from my hand, and one of them plunged a knife into my breast wounding a rib near the heart. However having recognised me, they carried me into the midst of the camp and asked me what I came for. I gave them to understand that the Illinois were under the protection of the King of France and of the Governor of the country and that I was surprised that they wished to break with the French, and not to continue at peace. All this time skirmishing was going on on both sides, and a warrior came to give notice that their left wing was giving way, and that they had recognised some Frenchmen among the Illinois, who shot at them. On this they were greatly irritated against me and held a council on what they should do with me. There was a man behind me with a knife in his hand, who every now and then lifted up my hair. They were divided in opinion. Tégantouki, chief of the Isonoutouan, desired to have me burnt. Agoasto, chief of the Onnoutagues, wished to have me set at liberty, as a friend of M. de la Salle, and he carried his point. They agreed that, in order to deceive the Illinois, they should give me a necklace of porcelain beads to prove that they also were children of the Governor, and ought to unite and make a good peace.

They sent me to deliver this message to the Illinois.
I had much difficulty in reaching them, on account
of the blood I had lost, both from my wound and
from my mouth. On my way I met the Fathers
Gabriel de la Ribourde and Zenoble Membré who
were coming to look after me. They expressed great
joy that these barbarians had not put me to death.
We went together to the Illinois, to whom I reported
the sentiments of the Iroquois, adding, however, that
they must not altogether trust them. They retired
within their village but seeing the Iroquois present
themselves every day in battle array they went to re-
join their wives and children, three leagues off. When
they went I was left with the two Recollets and three
Frenchmen. The Iroquois made a fort in their village, and left us in a cabin at some distance from their
fort. Two days after the Illinois appearing on the
neighbouring hills, the Iroquois thought that we had
some communication with them; this obliged them to
take us within their fort. They pressed me to return to the Illinois and induce them to make a treaty
of peace. They gave me one of their own nation as
a hostage and I went with Father Zenoble. The
Iroquois remained with the Illinois and one of the
latter came with me. When we got to the fort, instead of mending matters, he spoilt them entirely by
owning that they had in all only 400 men and that
the rest of their young men were gone to war,
and that if the Iroquois really wished for peace

they were ready to give them the beaver skins and some slaves which they had. The Iroquois called me to them and loaded me with reproaches; they told me that I was a liar to have said that the Illinois had 1,200 warriors, besides the allies who had given them assistance. Where were the 60 Frenchmen whom I had told them had been left at the village ? I had much difficulty in getting out of the scrape. The same evening they sent back the Illinois to tell his nation to come the next day to within half a league of the fort, and that they would there conclude the peace, which in fact they did at noon. The Iroquois gave them presents of necklaces and merchandise. The first necklace signified that the Governor of New France was angry at their having come to molest their brothers; the second was addressed to M. de la Salle with the same meaning; and the third, accompanied with merchandise, bound them as by oath to a strict alliance that hereafter they should live as brothers. They then separated and the Illinois believed, after these presents, in the sincerity of the peace, which induced them to come several times into the fort of Iroquois, where some Illinois chiefs having asked me what I thought, I told them they had everything to fear, that their enemies had no good faith, that I knew that they were making canoes of elm-bark, and that consequently it was intended to pursue them; and that they should take

c 2

advantage of any delay to retire to some distant nation for that they would most assuredly be betrayed.

The eighth day after their arrival, on the 10th of September, the Iroquois called me and the Father Zenoble to council, and having made me sit down, they placed six packets of beaver skins before us and addressing me, they said, that the two first packets were to inform M. de Frontenac that they would not eat his children and that he should not be angry at what they had done; the third, a plaster for my wound; the fourth, some oil to rub on my own and Father Zenoble's limbs, on account of the long journeys we had taken; the fifth, that the sun was bright;* the sixth, that we should profit by it and depart the next day for the French settlements. I asked them when they would go away themselves. Murmurs arose, and some of them said that they would eat some of the Illinois before they went away; upon which I kicked away their presents, saying, that I would have none of them, since they desired to eat the children of the Governor. An Abenakis who was with them, who spoke French, told me that I irritated them, and the chiefs rising drove me from the council. We went to our cabin where we passed the

---

* The published relation states:—"Par le cinqueme ils nous exhortaient à adorer le soleil" (p. 122). The original is simply:—"Le 5e quel e soleil etait beau."

night on our guard resolved to kill some of them before they should kill us, for we thought that we should not live out the night. However, at daybreak they directed us to depart, which we did. After five hours' sailing we landed to dry our peltries which were wet while we repaired our canoe. The Father Gabriel told me he was going aside to pray. I advised him not to go away, because we were surrounded by enemies. He went about 1,000 paces off and was taken by 40 savages, of a nation called Kikapous, who carried him away and broke his head. Finding that he did not return, I went to look for him with one of the men. Having disco-vered his trail, I found it cut by several others, which joined and ended at last in one. I brought back this sad news to the Father Zenoble, who was greatly grieved at it. Towards evening we made a great fire, hoping that perhaps he might return; and we went over to the other side of the river where we kept a good look out. Towards midnight we saw a man at a distance and then many others. The next day we crossed over the river to look for our crew and after waiting till noon we embarked and reached the Lake Illinois by short journeys, always hoping to meet with the good father. After having sailed on the lake as far as La Touissant we were wrecked, 20 leagues from the village of Poutouatamis. Our pro-visions failing us, I left a man to take care of our things and went off by land; but as I had a fever constantly on me and my legs were swollen, we did not arrive at this village till St Martin's day (November 11). During this journey we lived on wild garlick, which we were obliged to grub up from under the snow. When we arrived we found no savages: they were gone to their winter quarters. We were obliged to go to the places they had left, where we obtained hardly as much as two handful of Indian corn a-day and some frozen gourds which we piled up in a cabin at the water's side. Whilst we were gleaning a Frenchman whom we had left at the *cache*, came to the cabin where we had left our little store of provisions. He thought we had put them there for him, and therefore did not spare them. We were very much surprised as we were going off to Michilimakinac to find him in the cabin where he had arrived three days before. We had much pleasure in seeing him again, but little to see our provisions partly consumed. We did not delay to embark, and after two hours' sail, the wind in the offing obliged us to land when I saw a fresh trail and directed that it should be followed. It led to the Poutouatamis village, who had made a portage to the bay of the Puans. The next day, weak as we were, we carried our canoe and all our things into this bay, to which there was a league of portage. We embarked in Sturgeon Creek, and turned to the right at hazard, not knowing where to go. After sailing for a league we found a number of cabins, which led us to expect soon to find the savages. Five leagues from this place we were stopped by the wind for eight days, which compelled us to consume the few provisions we had collected together, and at last we were without anything. We held council, and despairing of being able to come up with the savages, every one asked to return to the village, where at least there was wood so that we might die waim. The wind lulling we set off, and on entering Sturgeon's Creek we saw a fire made by savages who had just gone away. We thought they were gone to their village and determined to go there; but the creek having frozen in the night we could not proceed in our canoe. We made shoes of the late Father Gabriel's cloak, having no leather. We were to have started in the morning, but one of my men being very ill from having eaten some *parre-fleche* in the evening delayed us. As I was urging our starting two Ottawas savages came up, who led us to where the Poutouatamis were. We found some Frenchmen with them, who kindly received us. I spent the winter with them, and the Father Zenoble left us to pass the winter with the Jesuits at the end of the bay. I left this place in the spring for Michilimakinac, hardly recovered from the effects of which we had suffered from hunger and cold during 34 days. We arrived at Michilimakinac about the *fete Dieu* in October. M. de la Salle arrived with M. Forest some days afterwards, on his way to seek us at the Illinois. He was very glad to see us again, and notwithstanding the many past reverses made new preparations to continue the discovery which he had undertaken. I therefore embarked with him for Fort Frontenac, to fetch things that we should want for the expedition. The Father Zenoble accompanied us. When we came to Lake Frontenac M. de la Salle went forward, and I waited for his boat at the village of Tezagon. When it arrived there I embarked for Illinois. At the Miamis River I assembled some Frenchmen and savages for the voyage of discovery, and M. de la Salle joined us in October. We went in canoes to the River Chicagou, where there is a portage which joins that of the Illinois. The rivers being frozen, we made sledges and dragged our baggage 30 leagues below the village of Illinois, where, finding the navigation open, we arrived at the end of January at the great River Mississippi. The distance from Chicagou was estimated at 140 leagues. We descended the river, and found, six leagues below, on the right, a great river,* which comes from the west, on which there are numerous nations. We slept at its mouth. The next day we went on to the village of Tamarous, six leagues off on the left. There was no one there, all the people being at their winter quarters in the woods. We made marks to inform the savages that we had passed,

* Missouri.

and continued our route as far as the River Ouabache,* which is 80 leagues from that of Illinois. It comes from the east, and is more than 500 leagues in length. It is by this river that the Iroquois advance to make war against the nations of the south. Continuing our voyage about 60 leagues, we came to a place which was named Fort Prudhomme, because one of our men lost himself there when out hunting, and was nine days without food. As they were looking for him they fell in with two Chikasas savages, whose village was three days' journey inland. They have 2,000 warriors, the greatest number of whom have *flat heads*, which is considered a beauty among them, the women taking pains to flatten the heads of their children, by means of a cushion which they put on the forehead and bind with a band, which they also fasten to the cradle, and thus make their heads take this form. When they grow up their faces are as big as a large soup plate. All the nations on the sea-coast have the same custom.

M. de la Salle sent back one of them with presents to his village, so that, if they had taken Prudhomme, they might send him back, but we found him on the tenth day, and as the Chikasas did not return, we continued our route as far as the village of Cappa, 50 leagues off. We arrived there in foggy weather, and as we heard the sound of the tambour we

---

* Ohio.

crossed over to the other side of the river, where, in less than half an hour, we made a fort. The savages having been informed that we were coming down the river, came in their canoes to look for us. We made them land, and sent two Frenchmen as hostages to their village; the chief visited us with the calumet, and we went to the savages. They regaled us with the best they had, and after having danced the calumet to M. de la Salle, they conducted us to their village of Toyengan, eight leagues from Cappa. They received us there in the same manner, and from thence they went with us to Toriman, two leagues further on, where we met with the same reception. It must be here remarked that these villages, the first of which is Osotonoy, are six leagues to the right descending the river, and are commonly called Akancas (Arkansas). The three first villages are situated on the great river (Mississippi). M. de la Salle erected the arms of the King there; they have cabins made with the bark of cedar; they have no other worship than the adoration of all sorts of animals. Their country is very beautiful, having abundance of peach, plum and apple trees, and vines flourish there; buffaloes, deer, stags, bears, turkeys, are very numerous. They have even domestic fowls. They have very little snow during the winter, and the ice is not thicker than a dollar. They gave us guides to conduct us to their allies, the Taencas, six leagues distant.

The first day we began to see and to kill alligators, which are numerous and from 15 to 20 feet long. When we arrived opposite to the village of the Taencas, M. de la Salle desired me to go to it and inform the chief of his arrival. I went with our guides, and we had to carry a bark canoe for ten *arpens*, and to launch it on a small lake in which their village was placed. I was surprised to find their cabins made of mud and covered with cane mats. The cabin of the chief was 40 feet square, the wall 10 feet high, a foot thick, and the roof, which was of a dome shaped, about 15 feet high. I was not less surprised when, on entering, I saw the chief seated on a camp bed, with three of his wives at his side, surrounded by more than 60 old men, clothed in large white cloaks, which are made by the women out of the bark of the mulberry tree and are tolerably well worked. The women were clothed in the same manner; and every time the chief spoke to them, before answering him, they howled and cried out several times— " O-o-o-o-o-o!" to show their respect for him, for their chiefs are held in as much consideration as our kings. No one drinks out of the chief's cup, nor eats out of his plate, and no one passes before him; when he walks they clean the path before him. When he dies they sacrifice his youngest wife, his house-steward (*maître d'hotel*), and a hundred men, to accompany him into the other world. They have a form of worship, and adore the sun. There is a

temple opposite the house of the chief, and similar
to it, except that three eagles are placed on this
temple who look towards the rising sun. The temple
is surrounded with strong mud walls, in which are
fixed spikes on which they place the heads of their
enemies whom they sacrifice to the sun. At the
door of the temple is a block of wood, on which is a
great shell (*vignot*), and plaited round with the hair of
their enemies in a plait as thick as an arm and about
20 fathoms (*toises*) long. The inside of the temple is
naked; there is an altar in the middle, and at the
foot of the altar three logs of wood are placed an
end, and a fire is kept up day and night by two old
priests (*jongleurs*), who are the directors (*maîtres*)
of their worship. These old men showed me a small
cabinet within the wall, made of mats of cane.
Desiring to see what was inside, the old men prevented me giving me to understand that their God
was there. But I have since learnt that it is the place
where they keep their treasure, such as fine pearls
which they fish up in the neighbourhood, and European
merchandise. At the last quarter of the moon all
the cabins make an offering of a dish of the best
food they have which is placed at the door of
the temple. The old men take care to carry it
away and to make a good feast of it with their
families. Every spring they make a clearing, which
they name " the field of the spirit," when all the
men work to the sound of the tambour. In the
autumn the Indian corn is harvested with much

ceremony and stored in magazines until the moon
of June in the following year, when all the village assemble, and invite their neighbours to eat it.
They do not leave the ground until they have eaten
it all, making great rejoicings the whole time. This
is all I learnt of this nation. The three villages
below have the same customs.

Let us return to the chief. When I was in his
cabin he told me with a smiling countenance the
pleasure he felt at the arrival of the French. I saw
that one of his wives wore a pearl necklace. I
presented her with ten yards of blue glass beads
in exchange for it. She made some difficulty, but
the chief having told her to let me have it, she
did so. I carried it to M. de la Salle, giving him
an account of all that I had seen and told him
that the chief intended to visit him the next day—
which he did. He would not have done this for
savages but the hope of obtaining some merchandise
induced him to act thus. He came the next day
with wooden canoes to the sound of the tambour and
the music of the women. The savages of the river
use no other boats than these. M. de la Salle
received him with much politeness, and gave him
some presents; they gave us, in return, plenty of
provisions and some of their robes. The chiefs
returned well satisfied. We stayed during the day,
which was the 22nd of March. An observation
gave 31° of latitude. We left on the 22nd, and slept
in an island ten leagues off. The next day we saw a

canoe, and M. de la Salle ordered me to chase it, which I did, and as I was just on the point of taking it, more than 100 men appeared on the banks of the river to defend their people. M. de la Salle shouted out to me to come back, which I did. We went on and encamped opposite them. Afterwards, M. de la Salle expressing a wish to meet them peacefully, I offered to carry to them the calumet, and embarking, went to them. At first they joined their hands, as a sign that they wished to be friends; I, who had but one hand, told our men to do the same thing.

I made the chief men among them cross over to M. de la Salle, who accompanied them to their village, three leagues inland and passed the night there with some of his men. The next day he returned with the chief of the village where he had slept who was a brother of the great chief of the Natches; he conducted us to his brother's village, situated on the hill side, near the river, at six leagues distance. We were very well received there. This nation counts more than 300 warriors. Here the men cultivate the ground, hunt and fish, as well as the Taencas, and their manners are the same. We departed thence on Good Friday, and after a voyage of 20 leagues, encamped at the mouth of a large river, which runs from the west. We continued our journey, and crossed a great canal, which went towards the sea on the right. Thirty leagues further on we saw some fishermen on the bank of the river, and sent to reconnoitre them. It was the village of the Quinipissas, who let fly their arrows upon our men, who retired in consequence. As M. de la Salle would not fight against any nation, he made us embark. Twelve leagues from this village, on the left, is that of the Tangibaos. Scarcely eight days before this village had been totally destroyed. Dead bodies were lying one on another and the cabins were burnt. We proceeded on our course, and after sailing 40 leagues, arrived at the sea on the 7th of April.

M. de la Salle sent canoes to inspect the channels, some of them went to the channel on the right hand, some to the left, and M. de la Salle chose the centre. In the evening each made his report, that is to say, that the channels were very fine, wide, and deep. We encamped on the right bank, we erected the arms of the King, and returned several times to inspect the channels. The same report was made. This river is 800 leagues long, without rapids, 400 from the country of the Scioux, and 400 from the mouth of the Illinois River to the sea. The banks are almost uninhabitable, on account of the spring floods.* The woods are all those of a boggy district, the

---

* The statement of De Tonty is thus altered in the published narrative :—

" The next day, the 27th of March, 1683, we encamped at the mouth of a great river coming from the west, and named

country one of canes and briars and of trees torn up by the roots ; but a league or two from the river, the most beautiful country in the world, prairies, woods of mulberry trees, vines, and fruits that we were not acquainted with. The savages gather the Indian corn twice in the year. In the lower part of the river, which might be settled, the river makes a bend N. and S., and in many places every now and then is joined by streams on the right and left. The river is only navigable [for large vessels ?] as far as the village of the Natches, for above that place the river winds too much; but this does not prevent the navigation of the river from the confluence of the Ouabache and the Mississippi as far as the sea. There are but few beavers, but to make amends, there is a large number of buffaloes, bears, large wolves—stags and hinds in abundance — and some lead mines, which yield two-thirds of ore to one of refuse. As these savages are stationary [*sedentaires*], and have some habits of

---

La Sablonniere. Ten leagues from hence, continuing our route, we found that the river divides itself into three channels. I took the one to the right, M. de la Foret that to the left, and M. de Salle the middle one. We each followed our course for about ten leagues, and found ourselves again in company at the junction of these branches of the river." The voyage is then represented to have continued until the 7th of April, when the party is stated to have arrived at the sea, and " to have found the river entering the Gulf of Mexico by a channel two leagues broad, deep, and very navigable."—*Dernière's Découvertes dans l'Amerique Septentrionale de la Salle*, pp. 188—193. Paris, 1697.

subordination, they might be obliged to make silk in order to procure necessaries for themselves; bringing to them from France the eggs of silkworms, for the forests are full of mulberry trees. This would be a valuable trade.

As for the country of Illinois, the river runs 100 leagues from the Fort St Louis, to where it falls into the Mississippi. Thus it may be said to contain some of the finest lands ever seen. The climate is the same as that of Paris, though in the 40° of latitude. The savages there are active and brave, but extremely lazy, except in war, when they think nothing of seeking their enemies at a distance of 500 or 600 leagues from their own country. This constantly occurs in the country of the Iroquois, whom, at my instigation, they continually harass. Not a year passes in which they do not take a number of prisoners and scalps. A few pieces of pure copper, whose origin we have not sought, are found in the river of the Illinois country. Polygamy prevails in this nation, and is one of the great hindrances to the introduction of Christianity, as well as the fact of their having no form of worship of their own. The nations lower down would be more easily converted, because they adore the sun, which is their divinity. This is all that I am able to relate of those parts.

Let us return to the sea coast, where, provisions failing, we were obliged to leave it sooner than we wished, in order to obtain provisions in the neighbouring villages. We did not know how to get anything from the village of the Quinipissas, who had so ill received us as we went down the river. We lived on potatoes until six leagues from their village, when we saw smoke. M. de la Salle sent to reconnoitre at night. Our people reported that they had seen some women. We went on at day-break and taking four of the women, encamped on the opposite bank. One of the women was then sent with merchandise to prove that we had no evil design and wished for their alliance and for provisions. She made her report. Some of them came immediately and invited us to encamp on the other bank, which we did. We sent back the three other women, keeping, however, constant guard. They brought us some provisions in the evening and the next morning, at day-break, the scoundrels attacked us.

We vigorously repulsed them, and by ten o'clock burnt their canoes, and, but for the fear of our ammunition failing, we should have attacked their village. We left in the evening in order to reach Natches where we had left a quantity of grain on passing down. When we arrived there the chief came out to meet us. M. de la Salle made them a present of the scalps we had taken from the Quinipissas. They had already heard the news, for they had resolved to betray and kill us. We went up to their village and as we saw no women there, we had no doubt of their having some evil design. In a moment we were surrounded by 1,500 men. They brought us something to eat, and we eat with our guns in our hands. As they were afraid of fire-arms, they did not dare to attack us. The chief begged M. de la Salle to go away, as his young men had not much sense, which we very willingly did—the game not being equal, we having only 50 men, French and savages. We then went on to the Taencas, and then to the Arkansas, where we were very well received. From thence we came to Fort Prudhomme, where M. de la Salle fell dangerously ill, which obliged him to send me forward, on the 6th of May, to arrange his affairs at Missilimakinac. In passing near the Ouabache, I found four Iroquois, who told us that there were 100 men of their nation coming on after them. This gave us some alarm. There is no pleasure in meeting warriors on one's road, especially when they have been unsuccessful. I left them and at about 20 leagues from Tamaraas we saw smoke. I ordered our people to prepare their arms, and we resolved to advance, expecting to meet the Iroquois. When we were near the smoke, we saw some canoes, which made us think that they could only be Illinois or Tamaraas. They were in fact the latter. As soon as they saw us, they came out of the wood in great numbers to attack us, taking us for Iroquois. I presented the calumet to them—they put down their arms and conducted us to their village without doing us any harm. The chiefs held a council, and, taking us for Iroquois, resolved

D

to burn us; and, but for some Illinois among us, we should have fared ill. They let us proceed. We arrived about the end of June, 1683 (1682), at the River Chicaou, and, by the middle of July, at Michilimakinac. M. de la Salle, having recovered, joined us in September. Resolving to go to France, he ordered me to collect together the French who were on the River Miamis to construct the Fort of St Louis in the Illinois. I left with this design, and when I arrived at the place, M. de la Salle, having changed his mind, joined me. They set to work at the fort, and it was finished in March, 1683.*

During the winter I gave all the nations notice of what we had done to defend them from the Iroquois, through whom they had lost 700 people in previous years. They approved of our good intentions, and established themselves, to the number of 300 cabins, near the Fort Illinois, as well Miamis as Chawanons.

M. de la Salle departed for France in the month of September, leaving me to command the fort. He met on his way the Chevalier de Bogis, whom M. de la Barre had sent with letters, ordering M. de la Salle to Quebec, who had no trouble in making the journey, as he was met with on the road. M. de la Salle wrote to me to receive M. de Bogis well, which I did. The winter passed, and on the 20th of March, 1684, being

---

* This date is no doubt correct, for there is a letter of La Salle's in existence, dated at Fort St Louis, April 2, 1683.

informed that the Iroquois were about to attack us we prepared to receive them, and dispatched a canoe to M. de la Durantaye, Governor of Missilimakinac, for assistance, in case the enemy should hold out against us a long time. The savages appeared on the 21st, and we repulsed them with loss. After six days' siege they retired with some slaves which they had made in the neighbourhood, who afterwards escaped and came back to the fort.

M. de la Durantaye, with Father Daloy, a Jesuit, arrived at the Fort with about 60 Frenchmen, whom they brought to our assistance, and to inform me of the orders of M. de la Barre, to leave the place. They stated that M. de Bogis was in possession of a place belonging to M. de la Forêt, who had accompanied M. de la Salle to France, and had returned by order of M. de la Salle with a *lettre de cachêt*. M. de la Barre was directed to deliver up to M. de la Forêt the lands belonging to the Sieur de la Salle, and which were occupied by others to his prejudice. He brought me news that M. de la Salle was sailing by way of the islands to find the mouth of the Mississippi, and had at court obtained a company for me. He sent me orders to command at Fort St Louis, as Captain of Foot and Governor. We took measures together, and formed a company of 20 men to maintain the Fort. M. de la Forêt went away in the autumn, for Fort Frontenac, and I began my journey to Illinois. Being stopped by the ice, I was obliged to halt at Montreal, where I passed the winter. When M. de la Forêt arrived there in the spring, we took new measures — he returned to Frontenac, and I went on to the Illinois, where I arrived in June (1685). M. le Chevalier de Bogis retired from his command according to the orders that I brought him from M. de la Barre.

The Miamis having seriously defeated the Illinois, it cost us 1,000 dollars to reconcile these two nations, which I did not accomplish without great trouble. In the autumn I embarked for Missilimakinac, in order to obtain news of M. de la Salle. I heard there that Monseigneur de Denonville had succeeded M. de la Barre ; and by a letter which he did me the honour to write to me, he expressed his wish to see me, that we might take measures for a war against the Iroquois, and informed me that M. de la Salle was engaged in seeking the mouth of the Mississippi in the Gulf of Mexico. Upon hearing this I resolved to go in search of him with a number of Canadians, and as soon as I should have found him, to return back to execute the orders of M. de Denonville.

I embarked, therefore, for the Illinois, on St Andrew's Day (30th of October, 1685); but being stopped by the ice, I was obliged to leave my canoe and to pro- ceed on by land. After going 120 leagues I arrived at the Fort of Chicaou, where M. de la Durantaye commanded; and from thence I came to Fort St Louis, where I arrived in the middle of January, 1685 (1686). I departed thence on the 16th February, with 30 Frenchmen and five Illinois and Chawanons, for the sea, which I reached in Holy Week. After having passed the above-named nations, I was very well received. I sent out two canoes, one towards the coast of Mexico, and the other towards Carolina, to see if they could discover anything. They each sailed about 30 leagues, but proceeded no farther for want of fresh water. They reported that where they had been the land began to rise. They brought me a porpoise and some oysters. As it would take us five months to reach the French settlements, I proposed to my men, that if they would trust to me to follow the coast as far as Manatte, that by this means we should arrive shortly at Montreal, that we should not lose our time, because we might discover some fine country and might even take some booty on our way. Part of my men were willing to adopt my plan; but as the rest were opposed to it, I decided to return the way I came.

The tide does not rise more than two feet perpendicularly on the sea coast, and the land is very low at the entrance of the river. We encamped in the place where M. de la Salle had erected the arms of the King. As they had been thrown down by the floods, I took them five leagues further up, and placed them in a higher situation. I put a silver *ecu* in the hollow of a tree to serve as a mark of time and place. We left this place on *Easter Monday*. When we came opposite the Quinipissas Village, the chiefs brought me the calumet and declared the sorrow they felt at the treachery they had perpetrated against me on our first voyage. I made an alliance with them. Forty leagues higher up, on the right, we discovered a village inland, with the inhabitants of which we also made an alliance. These are the Oumas, the bravest savages of the river. When we were at Arkansas, ten of the Frenchmen who accompanied me asked for a settlement on the River Arkansas on a seignory that M. de la Salle had given me on our first voyage. I granted the request to some of them. They remained there to build a house surrounded with stakes. The rest accompanied me to Illinois, in order to get what they wanted. I arrived there on St John's Day (24th of June). I made two chiefs of the Illinois embark with me in my canoe, to go and receive the orders of M. de Denonville, and we arrived at Montreal by the end of July.

I left that place at the beginning of October to return to the Illinois. I came there on the 10th of October, and I directly sent some Frenchmen to our savage allies to declare war against the Iroquois, inviting them to assemble at the Fort of Bonhomme, which they did in the month of April, 1686 (1687). The Sieur de la Forêt was already gone in a canoe with 30

Frenchmen, and he was to wait for me at Detroit till the end of May. I gave our savages a dog feast (*festin de chien*); and after having declared to them the will of the King and of the Governor, I left with 16 Frenchmen and a guide of the Miami nation. We encamped half a league from the Fort, to wait for the savages who might wish to follow us. I left 20 Frenchmen at the Fort and the Sieur de Bellefontaine to command there during my absence. Fifty Chaganons, four Loups, and seven Miamis came to join me at night; and the next day more than 300 Illinois came, but they went back again, with the exception of 149. This did not prevent my continuing my route; and after 200 leagues of journey by land, we came, on the 19th of May, to Fort Detroit. We made some canoes of elm, and I sent one of them to Fort St Joseph on the high ground above Detroit, 30 leagues from where we were, to give the Sieur Dulud, the Commander of this Fort, information of my arrival. The Sieur Beauvais de Tilly joined me, and afterwards the Sieur de la Forêt; then the Sieurs de la Durantaye and Dulud. I made the French and the savages coast along the bay. After Le Sieur Durantaye had saluted us, we returned the salute. They had with them 30 English, whom they had taken on the Lake Huron, at the place at which they had reached it. We made canoes on our journey, and coasted along Lake Erie to Niagara, where we made a fort below the portage to wait there for news. On our way we took 30 more

Englishmen, who were going to Missilimakinac, commanded by Major Gregory, who was bringing back
some Huron and Outawas slaves, taken by the
Iroquois. Had it not been for these two moves of
good luck our affairs would have turned out badly, as
we were at war with the Iroquois. The English,
from the great quantity of brandy which they had
with them, would have gained over our allies, and
thus we should have had all the savages and the
English upon us at once.

I sent the Sieur de la Forêt forward to inform M.
de Denonville of everything. He was at the Fort of
Frontenac, and he joined us at Fort Les Sables. The
large boat arrived, and brought us provisions. M.
le Monseigneur sent us word by it that he expected to
arrive by the 10th of July at the Marsh, which is
seven leagues from Sonnontouans.

The Poutouatamis, Hourons, and Ottawas joined us
there, and built some canoes. There was an Iroquois
slave among them whom I proposed to have put to
death for the insolent manner in which he spoke of
the French. They paid no attention to my proposal.
Five leagues on our march he ran away and gave information of our approach, and of the marks which
our savages bore to recognise each other, which did
us great harm in the ambuscade, as will be seen.

On the 10th we arrived at the Marsh of Fort Les
Sables and the army from below arrived at the same
time. I received orders to take possession of a certain

position, which I did with my company and savages. We then set about building a fort. On the 11th I went with 50 men to reconnoitre the road, three miles from the camp. On the 12th the Fort was finished, and we set off for the village. On the 13th, half a league from the prairie (*deserts*), we found an ambuscade, and my company, who were the advance guard, forced it. We lost seven men, of whom my lieutenant was one, and two of my own people. We were occupied for seven days in cutting the corn of the four villages. We returned to Fort Les Sables, and left it to build a fort at Niagara. From thence I returned to Fort St Louis with my cousin, the Sieur Dulud, who returned to his post with 18 soldiers and some savages. Having made half the portage, which is two leagues in length, some Hourons who followed us perceived some Iroquois, and ran to give us warning. There were only 40 of us, and as we thought the enemy strong, we agreed to fall back with our ammunition towards the Fort and get a reinforcement. We marched all night, and as the Sieur Dulud could not leave his detatchment, he begged me to go to the Marquis, while he lay in ambush in a very good position. I embarked, and when I came to the Fort, the Marquis was unwilling to give me any men, the more so as the militia was gone away and he had only some infantry remaining to escort him; however, he sent Captain Valiennes and 50 men to support us, who stayed at the portage whilst we crossed it. We embarked, and when clear of the land we perceived the Iroquois on the banks of the lake. We passed over, and I left the Sieur Dulud at his post at Detroit. I went on in company with the Reverend Father Crévier as far as Missilimakinac, and afterwards to Fort St Louis.

There I found M. Cavelier, a priest, his nephew, and the Father Anastatius, a Recollet, and two men. They concealed from me the assassination of M. de la Salle; and upon their assuring me that he was on the Gulf of Mexico in good health, I received them as if they had been M. de la Salle himself, and lent them more than 700 francs (28*l.*) M. Cavelier departed in the spring, 1687 (1688), to give an account of his voyage at court.

M. de la Forêt came here in the autumn, and went away in the following spring. On the 7th of April, one named Coutoure brought to me two Akansas, who danced the calumet. They informed me of the death of M. de la Salle, with all the circumstances which they had heard from the lips of M. Cavelier, who had fortunately discovered the house I had had built at Arkansas, where the said Coutoure stayed with three Frenchmen. He told me that the fear of not obtaining from me what he desired had made him conceal the death of his brother, but that he had told them of it.

M. Cavelier told me that the Cadadoquis had proposed to accompany him if he would go and fight against the Spaniards. He had objected, on account of there being only 14 Frenchmen. They replied that their nation was numerous, that they only wanted a few musqueteers, and that the Spaniards had much money, which they (the French) should take; and as for themselves, they only wished to keep the women and children as slaves. Coutoure told me that a young man whom M. Cavelier had left at Arkansas had assured him that this was very true. I would not undertake anything without the consent of the Governor of Canada. I sent the said Coutoure to the French remaining in Nicondiché, to get all the information he could. He set off, and at 100 leagues from the Fort was wrecked, and having lost everything returned.

In the interval M. de Denonville directed me to let the savages do as they liked, and to do nothing against the Iroquois. He at the same time informed me that war was declared against Spain. Upon this I came to the resolution of going to Naodiché, to execute what M. Chevalier had ventured to undertake, and to bring back M. de la Salle's men, who were on the sea coast not knowing of the misfortune that had befallen him. I set off on the 3rd of October, and joined my cousin, who was gone on before, and who was to accompany me as he expected that M. de la Forêt would come and take the command in my absence; but as he did not come I sent my cousin back to command the Fort.

I bought a boat larger than my own. We embarked five Frenchmen, one Chaganon, and two slaves. We arrived on the 17th at an Illinois village at the mouth of their river. They had just come from fighting the Osages, and had lost 13 men, but brought back 130 prisoners. We reached the village of the Kappas on the 16th of January, where we were received with demonstrations of joy, and for four days there was nothing but dancing, feasting, and masquerading after their manner. They danced the calumet for me, which confirmed the last alliance. On the 20th of January we came to Tongenga, and they wished to entertain us as the Kappas had done; but being in haste I deferred it until another time. I did the same with the Torremans, on my arrival on the 22nd. Leaving my crew I set off the next day for Assotoué, where my commercial house is. These savages had not yet seen me, as they lived on a branch of the river coming from the west. They did their best, giving me two women of the Cadadoquis nation, to whom I was going. I returned to Torremans on the 26th, and bought there two boats. We went away on the 27th. On the 29th, finding one of our men asleep when on duty as sentinel, I reprimanded him, and he left me. I sent two of my people to Coroa, to spare myself the fatigue of dragging on with our crew six leagues inland. The Frenchman, with whom I had quarrelled, made with them a third. We slept opposite the rivers of the Taencas, which run from Arkansas. They came there on the 2nd, this being the place of meeting. My Chaganon went out hunting on the other side of the river, where he was attacked by three Chacoumas. He killed one of them, and was slightly wounded by an arrow on the left breast. On the 4th the rest of the party arrived. On the 5th, being opposite Taencas, the men whom I had sent to Coroa not having brought any news of the two Frenchmen whom I was anxious about, I sent them to Natchés. They found that this nation had killed the two men. They retired as well as they could, making the savages believe that we were numerous. They arrived on the 8th of February. We set off on the 12th with 12 Taencas, and after a voyage of 12 leagues to the N.W. we left our boat and made 20 leagues portage, and on the 17th of February, 1690, came to Nachitoches. They made us stay at the place which is in the midst of the three villages called Nachitoches, Ouasita, and Capiché. The chiefs of the three nations assembled, and before they began to speak, the 30 Taencas who were with me got up, and leaving their arms went to the temple, to show how sincerely they wished to make a solid peace. After having taken their God to witness they asked for friendship. I made them some presents in the name of the Taencas. They remained some days in the village to traffic with salt, which these nations got from a salt lake in the neighbourhood. After their departure they gave me guides to Yatachés; and after ascending the river always towards the **N. W.** about 30 leagues, we found 15 cabins of Natchés, who received us pretty well. We arrived on the 16th of March at Yatachés, about 40 leagues from thence. The three villages of Yatachés, Nadas, and Choye are together. As they knew of our arrival they came three leagues to meet us with refreshments, and on joining us we went together to their villages. The chief made many feasts for us. I gave presents to them, and asked for guides to the Cadadoquis. They were very unwilling to give us any, as they had murdered three ambassadors about four days before, who came to their nation to make peace. However, by dint of entreaties, and assuring them that no harm would happen to their people, they granted me five men, and we got to Cadadoquis on the 28th. At the place where we were encamped we discovered the trail of men and horses. The next day some horsemen came to reconnoitre us, and after speaking to the wife of the chief whom I brought back with me, carried back the news. The next day a woman, who governed this nation, came to visit me with the principal persons of the village. She wept over me, demanding revenge for the death of her husband, and of the husband of the woman whom I was bringing back, both of whom had been killed by the Osages. To take advantage of everything I promised that their dead should be avenged. We went together to their temple, and after the priests had invoked their God

for a quarter of an hour they conducted me to the
cabin of their chief. Before entering they washed
my face with water, which is a ceremony among
them. During the time I was there I learnt from
them that 80 leagues off were the seven Frenchmen
whom M. Cavelier had left. I hoped to finish my
troubles by rejoining them, but the Frenchmen who
accompanied me, tired of the voyage, would go no
further. They were unmanageable persons over whom
I could exercise no authority in this distant country.
I was obliged to give way. All that I could do
was to engage one of them, with a savage, to accompany me to the village of Naovediché, where I hoped
to find the seven Frenchmen. I told those who
abandoned me, that to prevent the savages knowing
this, it was best to say that I had sent them away to
carry back the news of my arrival, so that the savages
should not suspect our disunion.

The Cadadoquis are united with two other villages
called Natchitoches and Nasoui, situated on the
Red River. All the nations of this tribe speak
the same language. Their cabins are covered
with straw, and they are not united in villages,
but their huts are distant one from the other.
Their fields are beautiful. They fish and hunt.
There is plenty of game, but few cattle (*bœufs*).
They wage cruel war with each other—hence their
villages are but thinly populated. I never found that
they did any work except making very fine bows,

which they make a traffic with distant nations. The Cadadoquis possess about 30 horses, which they call "cavali" (sp: *caballo*, a horse). The men and women are tattooed in the face, and all over the body. They call this river the *Red River*, because, in fact, it deposits a sand which makes the water as red as blood. I am not acquainted with their manners, having only seen them in passing.

I left this place on the 6th of April, directing our route southwards, with a Frenchman, a Chaganon, a little slave of mine, and five of their savages, whom they gave me as guides to Naouadiché. When I went away, I left in the hands of the wife of the chief a small box, in which I had put some ammunition. On our road we found some Naouadichès savages hunting, who assured me that the Frenchmen were staying with them. This gave me great pleasure, hoping to succeed in my object of finding them. On the 19th the Frenchman with me lost himself. I sent the savages who were with me to look for him. He came back on the 21st, and told me that, having lost our trail, he was near drowning himself in crossing a little river on a piece of timber. His bag slipped off, and thus all our powder was lost, which very much annoyed me as we were reduced to 60 pounds of ammunition. On the 23rd we slept half a league from the village and the chiefs came to visit us at night. I asked them about the Frenchmen. They told me that they had accompanied their chiefs to fight against the Spaniards seven days' journey off; that the Spaniards had surrounded them with their cavalry, and that their chief having spoken in their favour the Spaniards had given them horses and arms. Some of the others told me that the Quanouatins had killed three of them, and that the four others were gone in search of iron arrow heads : I did not doubt but they had murdered them. I told them that they had killed the Frenchmen. Directly all the women began to cry, and thus I saw that what I had said was true. I would not, therefore, accept the calumet. I told the chief I wanted four horses for my return, and having given him seven hatchets and a string of large glass beads, I received the next day four Spanish horses, two of which were marked on the haunche with an R and a crown (*couronne fermée*), and another with an N. Horses are very common among them. There is not a cabin which has not four or five. As this nation is sometimes at peace and sometimes at war with the neighbouring Spaniards, they take advantage of a war to carry off the horses. We harnessed ours as well as we could, and departed on the 29th, greatly vexed that we could not continue our route as far as M. de la Salle's camp. We were unable to obtain guides from this nation to take us there, though not more than 80 leagues off, besides being without ammunition, owing to the accident which I related before.

It was at the distance of three days' journey from

hence that M. de la Salle was murdered. I will say a few words of what I have heard of this misfortune. M. de la Salle having landed beyond the Mississippi, on the side of Mexico, about 80 leagues from the mouth of the river, and losing his vessels on the coast, saved a part of the cargo, and began to march along the sea-shore, in search of the Mississippi. Meeting with many obstacles on account of the bad roads, he resolved to go to Illinois by land, and loaded several horses with his baggage. The Father Anastatius, M. Cavelier, a priest, his brother; M. Cavelier, his nephew; M. Moranget, a relative; MM. Duhault and Lanctot, and several Frenchmen accompanied him, with a Chaganon savage. When three days' journey from the Naoudiché, and short of provisions, he sent Moranget, his servant, and the Chaganon, to hunt in a small wood with orders to return in the evening. When they had killed some buffaloes, they stopped to dry the meat. M. de la Salle was uneasy, and asked the Frenchmen who among them would go and look for them. Duhault and Lanctot had for a long time determined to kill M. de la Salle, because, during the journey along the sea-coast, he had compelled the brother of Lanctot, who was unable to keep up, to return to the camp: and who, when returning alone, was massacred by the savages. Lanctot vowed to God that he would never forgive his brother's death. As in long journeys there are always discontented persons,

he easily found partisans. He offered, therefore, with
them, to search for M. Moranget, in order to have an
opportunity to execute their design. Having found
the men, he told them that M. de la Salle was uneasy
about them; but the others showing that they could not
set off till the next day, it was agreed to sleep there. After
supper they arranged the order of the watch. It was
to begin with M. de Moranget; after him was to follow
the servant of M. de la Salle, and then the Chaganon.
After they had kept their watch and were asleep,
they were massacred, as persons attached to M. de la
Salle. At daybreak they heard the reports of pistols,
which were fired as signals by M. de la Salle, who
was coming with the Father Recollet in search of
them. The wretches laid wait for him, placing M.
Duhault's servant in front. When M. de la Salle came
near, he asked where M. Moranget was. The servant,
keeping on his hat, answered, that he was behind.
As M. de la Salle advanced to remind him of his
duty, he received three balls in his head, and fell
down dead. The Father Recollet was frightened, and,
thinking that he also was to be killed, threw himself
on his knees, and begged for a quarter of an hour to
prepare his soul. They replied that they were willing
to save his life. They went on together to where M.
Cavelier was, and, as they advanced, shouted, " Down
with your arms." M. de Cavelier, on hearing the
noise, came forward, and when told of the death of
his brother, threw himself on his knees, making

the same request that had been made by the Father Recollet. They granted him his life. He asked to go and bury the body of his brother, which was refused. Such was the end of one of the greatest men of the age. He was a man of wonderful ability, and capable of undertaking any discovery. His death much grieved the three Naoudichés whom M. de la Salle had found hunting, and who accompanied him to the village. After the murderers had committed this crime, they seized all the baggage of the deceased, and continued their journey to the village of Naoudichés, where they found two Frenchmen who had deserted from M. de la Salle two years before, and had taken up their abode with these savages.

After staying some days in this village, the savages proposed to them to go to war against the Quanoouatinos, to which the Frenchmen agreed, lest the savages should ill-treat them. As they were ready to set off, an English buccaneer, whom M. de la Salle had always liked, begged of the murderers that, as they were going to war with the savages, they would give him and his comrades some shirts. They flatly refused, which offended him, and he could not help expressing this to his comrades. They agreed together to make a second demand, and, if refused, to revenge the death of M. de la Salle. This they did some days afterwards. The Englishman, taking two pistols in his belt, accompanied by a Frenchman with his gun, went deliberately to the cabin of the murderers, whom they found were out shooting with bows and arrows. Lanctot met them and wished them good day, and asked how they were. They answered, " Pretty well, and that it was not necessary to ask how they did, as they were always eating turkeys and good venison." Then the Englishman asked for some ammunition and shirts, as they were provided with everything. They replied that M. de la Salle was their debtor, and that what they had taken was theirs. " You will not, then ?" said the Englishman. " No," replied they. On which the Englishman said to one of them, " You are a wretch ; you murdered my master," and firing his pistol killed him on the spot. Duhault tried to get into his cabin, but the Frenchman shot him also with a pistol in the loins, which threw him on the ground. M. Cavelier and Father Anastatius ran to his assistance. Duhault had hardly time to confess himself, for the father had but just given him absolution when he was finished by another pistol shot at the request of the savages, who could not endure that he should live after having killed their chief. The Englishman took possession of everything. He gave a share to M. Cavelier, who having found my abode in Arkansas, went from thence to Illinois. The Englishman remained at Naoudichés.

We reached Cadadoquis on the 10th of May. We stayed there to rest our horses, and went away on the 17th, with a guide who was to take us to the village of Coroas. After four days' journey he left us, in consequence of an accident which happened in crossing a marsh. As we were leading our horses by the bridle, he fancied he was pursued by an alligator, and tried to climb a tree. In his hurry he entangled the halter of my horse, which was drowned. This induced him to leave us without saying anything, lest we should punish him for the loss of the horse. We were thus left in great difficulty respecting the road which we were to take. I forgot to say that the savages who have horses use them both for war and for hunting. They make pointed saddles, wooden stirrups, and body-coverings of several skins, one over the other, as a protection from arrows. They arm the breast of their horses with the same material, a proof that they are not very far from the Spaniards. When our guide was gone I told the Chaganon to take the lead; all he said in answer was, that that was my business; and as I was unable to influence him, I was obliged to act as guide. I directed our course to the south-east, and after about 40 leagues' march, crossing seven rivers, we found the River Coroas. We made a raft to explore the other side of the river, but found there no dry land. We resolved to abandon our horses, as it was impossible to take them on upon account of the great inundation. In the evening, as we were preparing to depart, we saw some savages. We called to them in vain—they ran away, and we were unable to come up with them. Two of their dogs came to us, which, with two of our own, we embarked the next day on our raft, and left our horses. We crossed 50 leagues of flooded country. The water, where it was least deep, reached halfway up the legs; and in all this tract we found only one little island of dry land, where we killed a bear and dried its flesh. It would be difficult to give an idea of the trouble we had to get out of this miserable country, where it rained night and day. We were obliged to sleep on the trunks of two great trees placed together, and to make our fire on the trees, to eat our dogs, and to carry our baggage across large tracts covered with reeds; in short, I never suffered so much in my life as in this journey to the Mississippi, which we reached on the 11th of July. Finding where we were, and that we were only 30 leagues from Coroas, we resolved to go there, although we had never set foot in that village. We arrived there on the evening of the 14th. We had not eaten for three days, as we could find no animal, on account of the great flood. I found two of the Frenchmen who had abandoned me at this village. The savages received me very well, and sympathised with us in the sufferings we had undergone. During three days they did not cease feasting us, sending men out hunting every day, and not sparing their turkeys. I left them on the 20th, and reached Arkansas on the 31st, where I caught the fever, which obliged me to stay there till the 11th of August, when I left. The fever lasted until we got to the Illinois, in September.

I cannot describe the beauty of all the countries I have mentioned. If I had had a better knowledge of them, I should be better able to say what special advantages might be derived from them. As for the Mississippi, it could produce every year 20,000 *ecu's* worth of peltries, an abundance of lead, and wood for ship-building. A silk trade might be established there, and a port for the protection of vessels and the maintenance of a communication with the Gulf of Mexico. Pearls might be found there. If wheat will not grow at the lower part of the river, the upper country would furnish it; and the islands might be supplied with everything they need, such as planks, vegetables, grain, and salt beef. If I had not been hurried in making this narrative, I should have stated many circumstances which would have gratified the reader, but the loss of my notes during my travels is the reason why this relation is not such as I could have wished.

HENRY DE TONTY.

ACCOUNT

Of the Route from the Illinois, by the River
Mississippi, to the Gulf of Mexico.

Sir,

As the map accompanying this has been made
in haste, without proper calculations and measure-
ments, you may probably desire to make one; and for
this purpose I will state of the Mississippi that though
it winds much, we reckon from the Falls of St
Anthony to the sea eight hundred leagues, and you
perceive from the note that its direction is north and
south. The distance of the villages, reckoning from
the mouth of the river Illinois to the sea, or ascending from the sea as far as the river Quiouentagoet (on
the banks of which is a village containing eighty
Illinois cabins), is calculated at sixty leagues, and
from thence to the Miamis thirty leagues. The
Touraxouslins and Kikapous are fifteen leagues in
the interior, from the banks of the river; two hundred leagues from the junction of the river Illinois;
and from thence two hundred leagues to the Falls of
St Anthony. The rivers of the Missouri come from

E

the west, and after traversing three hundred leagues, arrives at a lake, which I believe *to be that of the Apaches.* The villages of the Missounta, Otenta, and Osage are near one another, and are situated in the prairies, one hundred and fifty leagues from the mouth of the Missouri. I should have stated before that the river of the Illinois is two hundred leagues in length. The Fort St Louis, with two hundred cabins, is seventy leagues from its mouth. The little river on which are the Machigama, Chipoussa, and Michibousa, is forty leagues from the Tamazoa. These tribes are situated about ten leagues from its mouth.

The mouth of the river of the Kasquinanipo is ten leagues from the mouth of the Ouabache. The village is situated seventy leagues upwards, on the bank of the river. The Maon, a numerous nation, and at peace with no one, is at the source of the said river, one hundred leagues from the Kasquinanipo. The Ozotoues are six leagues from the mouth of the river Arkansas. The Ionica, Yazou, Coroa, and Chonque, are, one with the other, about ten leagues from the Mississippi, on the river of the Yazou; the Sioux fifteen leagues above. All these villages are situated in prairies, but it is remarkable that the country about, the soil of which is the best in the world, and is intersected by streams, has been abandoned.

The Yazou are masters of the soil. The Mauton are seventy leagues from the Ossoztoues, and forty leagues from the Cadodoquis. The Coroa are their neighbours, though thirteen leagues off.

With respect to the other nations, I have sufficiently described at what distance they are from one another, from the nations on the Mississippi, and from those on the Red River, excepting the Nadouc, who are twelve leagues from the banks. In case the court wishes this discovery to be continued, I will add a note. In that I have stated it will be requisite to build a ship of fifty tons, to get to France from the Arkansas. Two pilots, &c.; particulars of every thing necessary, and more numerous than set forth in M. De la Salle's Note.

I undertake, with God's assistance, to descend the river, to take solar observations, to account for the expenses, and to sail to France with the said vessel built in the Arkansas. This is the place best adapted for the purpose, for we should not be interrupted by enemies; and wood, and everything necessary for subsistence, is there abundant.

HENRY DE TONTY.

ADDITIONAL STATEMENT OF WHAT WILL BE RE-
QUIRED FOR BUILDING THE VESSEL.

The former statement related to the expenses of the voyage, and presents for the savages. In case his Majesty grants the above request, I entreat Monseigneur de Pontchartrain to be kind enough to send orders to M. the Intendant at Rochefort to send the things to Messrs the Count de Frontenac and Champigny, and the latter to provide twenty large canoes and forty good men to manage them.

HENRY DE TONTY.

PETITION

Monseigneur,

Henry de Tonty humbly represents to your
Highness that he entered the army as a cadet, and
was employed in that capacity in the years 1638 and
1669 ; and that he afterwards served as a *garde marine* four years, at Marseilles and Toulon, and made
seven campaigns, that is, four on board ships of war,
and three in the galleys. While at Messina, he was
made captain-lieutenant to the *maître de camp* of
20,000. When the enemy attacked the post of
Libisso his right hand was shot away by a grenade,
and he was taken prisoner, and conducted to Metasse,
where he was detained six months, and then exchanged for the son of the governor of that place.
He then went to France, to obtain some favour from
his Majesty, and the King granted him three hundred
livres. He returned to the service in Sicily, made
the campaign as a volunteer in the galleys, and, when
the troops were discharged, being unable to obtain
employment he solicited at court, but being unsuc-

E

cessful, on account of the general peace, he decided, in 1678, to join the late Monsieur de la Salle, in order to accompany him the discoveries of Mexico, during which, until 1682, he was the only officer who did not abandon him.

These discoveries being finished, he remained, in 1683, commandant of Fort St Louis of the Illinois; and, in 1684, he was there attacked by two hundred Iroquois, whom he repulsed, with great loss on their side. During the same year he repaired to Quebec, at the command of M. de la Barre. In 1685 he returned to the Illinois, according to the orders which he received from the court, and from M. de la Salle, as a captain of foot in a Marine Detachment, and governor of Fort St Louis. In 1686 he went, with forty men in canoes, at his own expense, as far as the Gulf of Mexico, to seek for M. de la Salle. Not being able to find him there, he returned to Montreal, and put himself under the orders of Monsieur Denonville, to engage in the war with the Iroquois. On his return to the Illinois, he marched two hundred leagues by land, and as far in canoes, and joined the army, when, being at the head of a company of Canadians, he forced the ambuscade of the Tsonnonthouans.

The campaign being over, he returned to the Illinois, whence he departed, in 1689, to go in search of the remains of M. de la Salle's people; but, being deserted by his men, and unable to execute his design, he was compelled to relinquish it, when he had arrived within seven days' march of the Spaniards. Ten months were spent in going and returning. As he now finds himself without employment, he prays that, in consideration of his voyages, and heavy expenses, and considering also, that, during his service of seven years as captain, he has not received any pay, your Highness will be pleased to obtain for him, from his Majesty, a company, that he may coutinue his services in this country, where he has not ceased to harass the Iroquois, by enlisting the Illinois against them in his Majesty's cause.

And he will continue his prayers for the health of your Highness.

HENRY DE TONTY.

Nothing can be more true than the account given by the Sieur de Tonty in this petition; and should his Majesty reinstate the seven companies, which have been disbanded in this country, there will be justice in granting one of them to him, or some other recompense for the services which he has rendered, and which he is now returning to render, at Fort St Louis in the Illinois.

FRONTENAC.

REYNELL AND WEIGHT, LITTLE PULTENEY STREET.

ERRATA.

ON THE MISSISSIPPI.

Page 19, line 11, for " May," read " March."

  „ 87, „   8, for " 176," read " 1761."

IN DE TONTY'S NARRATIVE.

Page 45, line 20, after " river," add (ante pp. 20, 21).

  „ 50, „ 21, after " spring," add (1679).

  „ 53, „   9, after " 1679," add (1680).

  „ 60, „   3, after " Nov. 11," add (1680).

  „ 61, „ 25, after " spring," add (1681).

  „ 61, „ 28, after " October," add (June).

  „ 69, „ 11, after " April," add (1682).